T0365943

Behind
CLOSED DOORS

The Story of My Abusive Past.
The Memories Will Linger Forever.
I Have Forgiven But Will Never Forget.

R O S E   M A R ' R E E

ARCHWAY
PUBLISHING

Archway Publishing books may be ordered through booksellers or by contacting:

Archway Publishing
1663 Liberty Drive
Bloomington, IN 47403
www.archwaypublishing.com
844-669-3957

Because of the dynamic nature of the Internet, any web addresses or links contained in this book may have changed since publication and may no longer be valid. The views expressed in this work are solely those of the author and do not necessarily reflect the views of the publisher, and the publisher hereby disclaims any responsibility for them.

Any people depicted in stock imagery provided by Getty Images are models, and such images are being used for illustrative purposes only. Certain stock imagery © Getty Images.

ISBN: 978-1-6657-2436-4 (sc)
ISBN: 978-1-6657-2437-1 (e)

Library of Congress Control Number: 2022909588

Print information available on the last page.

Archway Publishing rev. date: 06/01/2022

Contents

Dedication

This book is dedicated to anyone who is currently in or has ever been in an abusive relationship. Don't give up hope. If I can make it out, so can you!

Acknowledgment

I would first like to thank my parents for helping me out of my abusive situation. Mom, dad, thank you for allowing me to gain my freedom back.

Next, I would like to thank my big sister, who inspired me so much and has also helped me get back on track once I was freed from the abuse I endured. I love you and thank you!

I would like to thank my editing team, who took the time out to make sure that this book was put together well. Lastly, I would like to say thank you to my publishing team, who, believed in me from day one and allowed me to tell my story so that I could spread awareness and help others just like myself.

Thank you!

About the Author

Rose Mar'Ree is a Black-American woman born and raised in Ohio. She was raised by her mom and step-dad, along with her older sister. Their biological father died when they were very young. Rose Mar'Ree and her oldest sister have half-siblings who are fraternal twins that they share with their biological father and a step-sister who they are very fond of as well. At the young age of seventeen, Rose started writing poetry after her great-grandmother passed away, who she also considered one of her best friends. Writing was a coping mechanism for her, and it helped her relieve the stress that comes with the pain of losing a loved one.

After developing a passion for writing poetry, it soon turned into writing songs, and eventually, it led to her aspirations of becoming a hip-hop artist. Rose Mar'Ree graduated Senior High School in 2003 and soon attended a Community College for the Recording and Arts program. Later on, in life, she graduated from the Community College in 2013 with a certificate in Phlebotomy. Rose is currently back in school and is preparing to get her Associates degree in Cyber Security.

She currently works as a secretary in a hospital in her hometown. She is also the owner of a cleaning company where she specializes in cleaning and disinfecting residential or commercial businesses, and she also has a business where she sells sunglasses and different apparels. Rose Mar'Ree is a single parent of a beautiful young lady who she attributes the reasoning behind speaking her truth and who inspires her to be a humble person, a hard worker, an optimist, and a dedicated mother every day. Besides writing, Rose Mar'Ree loves traveling, skating, bowling, going to the movies, go-kart racing, and hanging out with her closest family and friends.

Behind Closed Doors is her first published novel, in which she shares her experience being in a three-year abusive relationship.

With support from her family and friends, Rose Mar'Ree dedicates her life to helping others who may be facing abuse in their relationships.

Introduction

Since I broke up with my past significant other, more than a decade has passed. Sometimes I wish our story had turned out differently. Please don't get me wrong, I have moved on from it, from everything, and I do not in any way miss him or any part of whatever we had. However, you should understand how tough it can be to forget your first love, even if he is a conman, a liar, a thief, and an abuser. Love can be hell sometimes, especially when chained to a tormentor.

My ex-love was not such a devil at times but loving him was hell. I still dream of the nights he made me cry and the days he made me consider suicide just to get out of this life. I was everything he needed and wanted me to be. I was strong sometimes, and I played weak when he needed me to. I was the good girl he had always told me he wanted, but yet he mistreated me.

We met in the most unexpectedly way, and I thought that this must be it. He was the one. I felt that our relationship would last for a lifetime. I wish I knew better about love or the heart of men. I wish I had listened to my older sister when she told me not to date him. But who would blame me? I was young and naive, so he took advantage of that, and I fell for his lies.

Ready?

Was I really ready or just too young to know any better? I let this man into my world and just went for the ride. As I stare off into space, looking puzzled and dazed, I am still confused in so many ways. I know now that it was wrong, but it felt so right. While thinking that age is nothing more than a number, he insisted that I realize and accept it, so I did, and those became my feelings initially.

Chapter 1

It all began back in 2005. I was still living with my parents, and I decided to enroll in a community college. The classes started sometime in August. The school became my main focus at that moment. That same year I started going to the gym for fitness training, and at that time, they were offering aerobics classes, so I decided to join. I was twenty-one years old at the time and taking courses with older ladies. Aerobics seemed like something interesting to do, and the instructor made it a lot of fun and made me feel comfortable. He would bring his wife to the gym to assist on different occasions.

Fast forward to 2006, I wasn't going to the gym anymore because I didn't have the time or the money to continue, so I gave it up. On February 14, 2006, I decided to straighten up my room a little bit. While I was cleaning, I came across a business card from the man who had taught the aerobics class at the gym that I used to attend. I tossed the card in the trash and didn't think any more about it. Two days later, I was on my way, driving to school. As I came to a stop at the stop sign, I happened to look in my rearview mirror. Someone in a white vehicle kept flashing their lights at me. The whole time, I was thinking, who could this be? What is going on?

As I continued to drive off and came to another stop sign, the vehicle was still behind me, flashing its lights. All of a sudden, the car, which turned out to be a white limousine, pulled up beside me, rolled down the window, and signaled for me to pull over. As I looked closer, I noticed it was the aerobics instructor whose business card I had just found and tossed days earlier. I drove off from the stop sign and pulled over to the side of the road. He proceeded to get out of his vehicle.

He walked up to my car with the biggest smile and said, "Hey you! Give me a hug!"

I stepped out and hugged him. We talked for a little bit. He wanted to know where and how I had been.

I replied, "I've been good," and left it at that. He said, "Do you know that I have been looking for you for quite some time now?" At that moment, the only thing I was thinking in my head was, 'Why? Aren't you married?' But it was a possibility that they weren't together anymore. He asked where I was headed, and I told him that I was headed to school, as I had started taking some college courses. He said, "Okay," and the next moment asked for my phone number. I didn't hesitate. I gave him my phone number, after which he gave me the biggest hug ever and said that he would call me that evening.

Later that night, I was eating dinner when the aerobics instructor called me at around 7:30 pm; I was a little nervous, so I did not answer the phone. After I finished eating, I got myself together and called him back. He answered the phone in a whispering tone and said, "Give me a minute, and I'll call you right back."

I replied, "Okay," but wondered why he was whispering. Was he hiding something?

Around 8:30 pm, he called me back, and we talked on the phone almost the whole night. I noticed that he was such a smooth talker; I enjoyed his personality. He was definitely a charmer. After about a week, as we continued to converse, he eventually asked me out on a date.

I said, "I thought you were married? I remember meeting your wife at the gym."

He told me they were separated, but he was still living in the house, and they were sleeping in separate bedrooms until he found a place of his own.

I inquired, "Why? What happened?"

He told me he had wanted to have a child with her, but she had refused because she already had two girls from her previous marriage. The youngest of her daughters had a disability and could not walk, and as a result, she was wheel-chair bound. His wife had to spend a lot of time caring for her daughter's needs, so she didn't think it would be wise to have more children. He also mentioned that his oldest stepdaughter was my age as well. I was shocked.

He then told me that he was forty-four years old and that he had been falsely accused of armed robbery, for which he had gone to prison for eight and a half years. He had gone into a liquor store after he'd gotten off work to buy a beer. Although he had given the cashier a twenty-dollar bill, the cashier had not given him his change back. An argument ensued, and he had reached into the drawer to grab the money that was owed to him, and that's why he was arrested and later convicted of armed robbery. I wasn't sure if I believed his story, but I did not question it.

Still in disbelief, I took him up on his offer. I knew that it was not a good idea to be dating a much older man who was still married and just so happened to be around the same age as my parents. I decided to do it anyway just to see what he had to offer since he seemed honest enough at the time, and he was working on getting divorced. We went out a couple of times.

I told him that I was heavy into hip-hop music and that I liked to write and rap my own songs. I let him listen to a demo CD that I had recorded at the music studio. He enjoyed my music. He said that he knew a guy who could help me further my music career. He introduced us, and the guy liked what he heard and said, "We were going to hook up and do some stuff together, but we never did."

I found out later that the reason I never saw the guy again was because he owed my dude, I was dating some money and never paid my dude back. So, he told me that he stopped dealing with the guy because of that.

After two weeks of dating regularly, he asked me if I could go out of town with him because he needed to take care of some business. I did. I really enjoyed his company and the time we spent together. He made me feel extra special. We stayed at an inn for a couple of days, and that is where we made love for the first time. He was the only guy I had been intimate with at that time. I was scared and nervous about going through it, but I eventually relaxed. It felt as though we had known each other forever. I guess that is what love feels like at the beginning of a relationship.

I really enjoyed our time together and grew attached to him very quickly, to the point I started getting jealous every time he went home to his wife. He reassured me that nothing was going on between them, and it was just somewhere for him to live temporarily. They were on good terms, still speaking and acknowledging one another. She was a school teacher, and he would go up to the school to help her out around the classroom.

When I'd tell him that I thought he didn't want to be with her anymore, he would reply, "I don't. I just do not want us to be sour toward each other just because our marriage didn't work out the way that we had planned." She had no idea that I was involved with her soon-to-be ex-husband.

He told me that he had gotten married to her before he'd gone to jail, and they had been married for ten years; He wanted them to end things on good terms because he still cared about her feelings and cared deeply for his stepchildren as well as the dog they shared together. He also reminded me when he'd gone to jail and done eight and a half years, she had stood by his side through it all.

How double-dog dare you put your hands on me? You are not my daddy nor my mother, not even my granny, for that matter. This is far beyond any level of insanity. Are you crazy? I didn't think that you were until putting your hands on me took things to a whole new level. "Respect me." This is not what love is about. Why are you trying to control me?

Chapter 2

Moving forward, I started working a job at a hotel down-town in my hometown a month after my newfound love, and I started dating. It was my first real job after grad-uating from senior high school. He had his limousine business that was a little rocky to start off, so it wasn't bringing in much money. He wanted to move from where he had been living so badly. He wanted me to come to his place so that we could start to build on our relationship.

He knew that his wife would have the money he needed to start over fresh, but she wouldn't just give it to him quickly. He had spoken with her about letting him have the money, but she said she would help him out only if they were intimate one last time. He asked me if that would be alright for him to do without me feeling some type of way about it. I was totally against it, but he talked me into letting him do it by telling me how we would be able to be together and happier a lot sooner. I was very naive and had started to fall in love with this man, so I gave in and agreed to it.

How could I allow this man to manipulate my mind so much? But yet, I fell for it every time. I was mad at myself for allowing things to get out of control. I consented to this; how could I be so stupid, I kept asking myself?

I was becoming more jealous, although I never really considered myself a jealous-hearted kind of person. I was constantly calling and texting him on his cell phone. He would text back and tell me to calm down, he was still with his wife, and he'd call me as soon as they were done. At that point, I was furious, but I should not have consented to it to begin with.

I agreed without fully thinking when he asked for my permission. When I finally talked to him, I asked sarcastically, "Well did you enjoy it?" He replied, "No, I didn't," but of course, I knew that was a lie. He said she was going to write him a check for fifteen hundred dollars. Surprisingly, to me, she actually did what he said she would do.

After he cashed the check, I went with him to look for a new place to stay. I asked him how he would continue to pay rent with no income. He told me to let him worry about that. He was good at coming up with solutions to his problems.

It was prom season for high school teens, and his aunt owned a bridal shop where she made dresses and sold accessories to prom and wedding-goers. They decided to join forces and do business together. That way, when people come into the shop to look for prom or wedding dresses, they have the option to rent a limousine as well as a package deal.

I tried helping by making flyers. My sister disapproved of our relationship, but she was willing to help me help him. I posted the flyers around the neighborhood, at different locations, and inside the stores. I was so invested in this relationship. I jumped in feet first, too fast and too deep. I did not think about the future; I was just so happy to have a serious relationship with someone. My lover's age never crossed my mind. He was a great catch that I had caught.

Sometime during June of 2006, he finally moved out of the house he shared with his wife. I was so excited that I went to his wife's house while she was at work to help him move all his things to the new place. As I am older and more mature, I know now that I was wrong; I should not have been in a relationship with him or at his wife's home at all. I feel as though I let this man brainwash me into his crazy world.

After he moved and got situated, we became even closer as time went on. I went from staying the night once or twice a week to basically living with him every day. After about a month of being so close to one another, we began to bump heads naturally, and things didn't seem perfect anymore. Eventually, he just got comfortable enough with me being there that he began to smoke and drink alcohol daily, then he started talking recklessly towards me. I experienced my first dose of abuse from him, which I didn't expect, but this was just the beginning.

He mentioned to me that he sells all types of substances just to make enough money to live off of, and he is only the supplier. I was against the whole selling thing when he told me. I didn't want to believe that he was into that type of lifestyle, but I loved him, so I accepted that this is what he does.

One day while he was sitting on the sofa, he said, "I have this substance that I need to try out before selling it." He wanted me to perform something sexual on him while he tried it out, and he wanted to record it all simultaneously on his video camera. I did not want to, and I especially did not want to be filmed doing it. I said, "NO!" He grabbed my arm and yanked me down to his level. I stood back up and said, "Don't you ever put your hands on me again," and he apologized. At that moment, I didn't know what to think because it all happened so fast that I didn't get a chance to gather my thoughts.

That was one of many apologies. I endured this type of behavior, believing that he could change or would change for me, but I was wrong. My guy could be a sweetheart at times, but it seemed that his demons always got the best of him. He told me stories of him having to take anger management classes to help him learn how to control his temper. He often would put his hands on his first ex-wife, so by the time he remarried, he did not attempt to put his hands on his second wife because she had three brothers; one who was an attorney and the other two who were police officers. He knew what would happen in that relationship.

Like most women, we think that we can change a man for the better and not treat us as badly as the other women they disrespected in their life. That isn't the case most of the time. Things only worsen when we allow it to happen, and they continue to get away with it.

I was scared the first time it happened, and I did not know what to think. This was my first serious adult relationship. I had never experienced any type of mental or physical abuse. When he apologized, I honestly thought he would not do it again and was genuinely sorry.

As time passed, he and I would have these full-blown arguments about me having a baby with him to the point it would stress me out.

I was young, and I never wanted kids at all. Watching my sister raise my niece alone was enough. I did not want to have to go through that myself.

He would say things to me like he should not have to wear protection when we have intercourse because he did not like how it felt.

The doctor I was consulting offered me many different birth control protection to guard against me getting pregnant since I didn't want children. He was against any form of birth control that my doctor offered.

He would get mad and state that I didn't need things like that. Things had gotten so bad between us that I could not focus on school anymore. I would fall asleep in my classes all the time, and I started failing, then I just stopped going to school completely. I became stressed, depressed and tired. This relationship took a lot out of me. I was not eating, so my energy was drained. I was losing a lot of weight from being so stressed out to the point my parents started to really worry about me and my lifestyle with this man.

My parents did not like him at all. My father felt like he was using me and just trying to show me off and show people how he could get this young girl. My sister said, "Can't no old man do anything for you but give you worms and steal your youth." We laughed a bit; my sister is hilarious at times. I thought she was just joking like we always do together, but it was true, and later on, as the relationship continued, she was right about one thing: he was stealing my youth in many ways.

The limousine business wasn't doing good. After prom season was over, everything started falling apart. He was not able to book clients for weddings either, and other than him dealing, he had to come up with a plan B to make an honest living, so he could continue to pay rent and pay all his other bills.

Transportation was limited for him. The car he had was acting up and needed a lot of things fixed. He did not want to drive his limousine around town. I no longer had my car. It was old and needed a lot of work done to it, so I had to get rid of it. Once again, my guy thought that his only option was asking his wife for help. She helped him by picking him up from his place and drive to her job, then she would let him use her vehicle all day to take care of his business as far as applying for jobs and such.

Later, he would pick her back up from her job, and she would drop him back off at home, which began to be an everyday thing. I did not like that he was using her vehicle, but I couldn't help him out either. One of those many days of him using her vehicle, I called him, but he did not answer. When he returned my call, I immediately answered and asked, "Where were you?" His wife was on the other end of the receiver, and she said, "Leave my husband alone." Surprised and nervous, I hung the phone up on her. My cell phone rang an hour later, and I almost did not answer because I thought it was his wife again. It was him saying how he had forgotten and left his cell phone in her car, so I mentioned how she had returned a phone call that I had placed to him, and she told me to leave him alone. He said, "I will get on her that we aren't together anymore, so I don't know why she is acting like that."

My mom bought herself a new car and gave me her old one so that I would have transportation. I allowed him to drive the car so that his wife didn't need to be involved in his life. He would drop me off at work and pick me back up every day. Once I really started living with this man and began experiencing the struggles with him, I noticed that he was heavy into drinking alcohol. He hid the drinking from me for a while. I did not know that he was becoming an alcoholic, or he might have been an alcoholic all this time. I just was unaware of it, and it did not even smell on him.

Things were starting to unfold as time went on. He did not drink alcohol around me at all before. Maybe he felt more comfortable after I moved in for sure, he could have been stressed out about his circumstances, or he just got tired of hiding his authentic self from me. Who really knows? Eventually, what's done in the dark shall come to light, or so I've heard. Soon everything else he was capable of that I was unaware of came into play.

It started with him just having a beer once a week, to him drinking a pint of gin every day, to him just getting out of hand and becoming intolerable with this habit. Drinking had turned into an addiction for him. It had gotten so bad that he began waking up drinking, going to bed drinking, and drinking while he was driving. All this drinking became such a problem for our relationship.

I wasn't a drinker; I told him how I felt about him drinking so often and how I had family members who were violent alcoholics. He decided he would not drink as much as he had been, but he would not stop drinking completely. He found employment at a local restaurant, then became close with one of his new co-workers, and they instantly became buddies. He would hang out with him and his girlfriend every chance they could when they weren't at work. Unbeknownst to me, his co-worker was also a heavy drinker, and he got into different substances every so often just as well.

I did not like that they hung out together after I found out this information because they would constantly drink enough to get DRUNK.

His drinking buddy eventually died from an overdose, and he took this news very badly. He said he couldn't continue to work at that restaurant, so he found another job as a pizza delivery driver somewhere else. He would still continue to drink a lot even while he was supposed to be driving the company vehicle to deliver pizza to customers.

We would constantly argue about his bad drinking habit. I told him that he was an alcoholic, a monster, and not the man that I thought I knew. He denied it, of course, like most alcoholics who are in denial. On occasion, when we would go to his father's house, they would take a shot of whisky together and drink moonshine that his father had gotten from Alabama. That's when I found out that his parents also drank a lot and that his mother had died from liver cirrhosis from excessive drinking. I never met his mother. She had passed away while serving his eight and a half years prison sentence before we met.

This man continued to convince me to have a baby with him. He wanted to give his father a biological grandchild so badly. His father already had a non-biological grandson. His parents had adopted a little girl when she was just 2 years old, now grown, she had a son. He told me he and his adopted sister weren't friends for a long time because she had accused him of raping her. He said she made the whole thing up and that she had a tumor in her head and a few surgeries that messed her mind up, and I believed him. We continued to discuss how I felt about having a baby. "I'm not ready yet, I'm just not ready to be a mom, and I don't think I ever want to be a mom," I said. I said to him, "Please stop pressuring me."

He said he did not understand why I didn't want a child. He also said that was the whole purpose of wanting to divorce his wife because she did not want any more children, and he just wanted one of his own.

I was hiding a secret from him. I had held onto something for a long time before we met and was too scared to act on it. He did not know that I had always wanted to be in a relationship with a female. I would fantasize about being with a woman, but I was ashamed, so I was with him because I didn't know how or when to come out of the closet. Me being a lesbian would not have been accepted. I hid it from everyone, my family, friends, even my best friend, who was actually a gay male. I had never been with a woman before; all I knew was that I was very much attracted to them.

I was the good girl my guy wanted, and he was attracted to that. I fell in love with him because of his amazing personality, sense of humor, and his gift for good conversation. He could talk you into doing just about anything. That was one of his many talents. I guess that is why I fell for it all the time. I never really imagined being with a male, although I had a boyfriend in senior high school. When I was about 14 or 15 years old, we started dating, and his mom adored me. We dated off and on for four years and also went to prom together. I felt like I had been living a lie my whole life. I just did not know how or when to break loose from my shell.

Blind

A deer in headlights blinded by the love life. I shouldn't have to fist-fight to show my love; that's not right. When love is truly real, is this how it's supposed to make you feel? – Sick to your stomach; is love supposed to make you ill? So caught up in your own mind, believing what he says all the time, brainwashing you is a sign; how could love be so blind?

A few months down the road, about 7 months into our relationship, I made the terrible mistake of letting myself get pregnant. I gave up and gave in to his selfishness and gave him what he said he had wanted so much. He hoped for a daughter, "Daddy's little girl," he would say. Once I got pregnant, it felt so wrong; he was happy, me, not so much. I was disappointed with myself.

I kept asking myself how we were going to support a baby with barely any money. Or even raise a baby when we were constantly at each other's throat. I did not want that for my child. I told him that things had to start getting better because we were about to become parents. He agreed and promised that he would try, yet, once again, I believed his lies. A couple of my co-workers, who I confided in, told me that I should not let him talk me into having a baby, but I did not listen. I loved him, and I convinced myself that this was the right thing to do.

As time went on, this man became more possessive. If I did not do what he wanted me to do, that's when he would disrespect me, call me disrespectful names, put his hands on me, or kick me out of his house. Things had gotten to the point of no return, and I was contemplating suicide. I would walk down to the river behind our apartment and stand there on the rocks, thinking about jumping to death. He brought my self-esteem to an all-time low. I didn't love myself anymore. With no one to really talk to, I was hurting inside and wondering why this man who claimed to love me would continue to hurt me. Our arguments would get so uncontrollably bad.

One night while he was driving, we got into another stupid argument about him accusing me of cheating on him with some guy I worked with, and I exploded. I don't know why, but I grabbed the steering wheel and started shifting the gears while the car was in motion, trying to make us crash. Then, I just blacked out.

When I came back to my senses, I didn't remember what all had happened, although I do remember us arguing and me grabbing the steering wheel. Needless to say, we made it home safe, but I was still upset. I told him that I am not a cheater and asked him, "What would make you think that I am cheating on you anyway?" He couldn't answer. This was just another one of his acts of getting under my skin; it's like he enjoyed arguing with me for no reason at all.

Moving along, three months into my pregnancy, I did not do what he wanted me to do. Hence, he cursed me out of my name right then, and I knew I should not have this baby. I did not want to bring a child into this world when things between us were not working out, so I ended our relationship. I could no longer deal with this nonsense, so I decided to get rid of the baby. My father loaned me some money to have an abortion, and my sister took me to the abortion clinic.

I did not tell him that I was going to abort our child. He kept calling me, leaving messages apologizing, and I was trying not to get taken in. I ignored his calls for about three weeks. I had the abortion, and my sister was supposed to take me back to the clinic in 6 weeks for a follow-up to make sure everything had healed up properly. I did feel bad about aborting this child without talking to him about it first, but I felt I had no choice. He would have tried talking me out of it, making me feel bad about not wanting the baby or just about anything to change my mind.

After the three weeks of not talking to him, I gave in and listened to what he had to say. He apologized for how he had been treating me and said it would never happen again. He swore on his mother's grave, and since he was a church-going man, he told me that he was not raised that way. I couldn't help but think about all those times he told me how he had gotten physically abusive with his first ex-wife and underwent anger management classes with his second wife to control his anger, but for some reason, I didn't think he would be the same way toward me.

Yet, it still happened. I said, "Look! You have really hurt me. How can you say that you love me? You were cursing me out of my name, trying to control me, and putting your hands on me, which isn't love - it's abuse." He replied, "You are absolutely right. What kind of man am I? I was dead wrong for everything, and I know you don't want to continue to hear me apologize for my actions, but I am sorry for causing you so much pain. At times I get stressed out and allow my anger to take over." I said, "I get stressed out as well, but I do not take my anger out on you!" I told him that I had gotten rid of the baby, and he was upset, but he agreed that it really was not the right time to bring a baby into this world.

We talked for a while and made up, so I ended up forgiving him and decided to give our relationship another chance. He actually turned out to be the one who took me to my follow-up appointment at the abortion clinic. They told me everything had healed up good, but I was still in lots of pain, physically and emotionally. They told me that it was normal and just prescribed me more medication to take for my pain and told me that maybe I should talk to someone to help me cope with the procedure.

Love is so blind; how could I see what was coming next? As the next weeks went on, he was creeping back into his old ways. He started disrespecting me once again and this time blaming me for killing our unborn child, telling me I'm the reason our child isn't here, lowering my self-esteem more than ever.

I kept asking myself, why do I continue to stay and forgive this man over and over again? Was love that blind? It was so hard to escape this abuse I was in that it felt like I had become numb to it. It is just so hard to completely walk away from someone you truly love. I tried and found myself right back into the same predicament.

Growing up, I remember watching the Maury Talk Show on television, watching women talk about being in an abusive relationship with their boyfriend/husband, and me saying, "Why won't they just leave? Walk away!" I would be yelling at the television screen, saying, "I will never get myself into a situation like that, and I will never let a man put his hands on me." Now I understand why it was so hard for them. I realized it's not that easy when you're in the driver's seat going through the exact situation. I learned 2 things; to never say never, and to never judge a book by its cover, because you just do not know when it may happen to you. It can be hard to know what someone else is dealing with or what's going on in their mind.

He no longer wanted to work as a pizza delivery driver as it was not bringing in enough money, but he could not get a better job because he had a felony on his record. Plus, he said that he missed being in the gym and teaching aerobics classes. Since I wanted to be a musician, the ATL was the place to be if you wanted to get noticed.

I asked him if he wanted to move there for better opportunities. He told me, "Yeah!" and he said, as a matter of fact, he had an old friend that he grew up with that lived there. His friend was retired, but he was going to reach out and contact him to see if he could help him look for a job at one of the fitness centers out that way. His friend contacted him back and said that he worked out at one of the biggest gyms there and that he was good friends with the general manager. His friend told him that he would ask the general manager about a position there for him. His friend talked with the general manager, who responded, "If he can get here, he got the job." What a joyous feeling we had, thinking that hopefully, things would finally start looking up for him and begin getting better between us.

During June of 2007, we were selling everything we could so that we could pack up and move out of town. He suggested that I get a better vehicle from a car dealership since the one my mom gave me was not in great shape so that we could have a decent driving vehicle to go to Georgia in.

He said that a guy he knew, his father was the GM (general manager) at a Toyota car dealership, and he might give me a good deal on a car. We went to the dealership, talked to the guy, and he did give me a good deal on a Toyota Camry with low mileage and a reasonable car note. I was happy; they even took a picture of us in front of my newly owned vehicle. Once I got my new vehicle, I sold my old car for a measly $500 dollars.

We posted an ad in the local newspaper about our yard sale. Although we were living together, I still had all my belongings at my parents' house. I went to my parents' house to clean my bedroom and to gather all the things that I wanted to sell at the yard sale and the things I didn't need any longer; I just threw them all away in the trash.

Once I was finished at my parents' house, I returned back to my boyfriend's house with the things I wanted to sell along with the things that I wanted to take out of town with me. When I saw him, I noticed he was in a bad mood; his behavior and tone were way off. I asked, "What's wrong with you?" He said, "Don't come back here starting drama," I started looking confused. "Huh!" I said, "What are you talking about? All I asked was, what's wrong with you? When I left to go get my belongings from my parents' house, everything was good with us now I come back, and things once again goes bad." He jumped up in rage and told me to get out of his house, cursing and yelling at me.

He opened the door and threw all my stuff in the hallway, including everything for the yard sale that I had brought from my parents' house. I was in disbelief, and my feelings were hurt.

I gathered all my things up, took them back to my car, and sat there, crying my eyes out for a while. I was really upset, very offended, and did not understand what had just happened. We were happy and just discussed the yard sale that morning before I left to go get everything from my parents' house.

The plan was that I was going to go collect all my stuff from my parents' house that I wanted to get rid of, and now this attitude of his came completely out of thin air. I didn't want to go back to my parents' house since they had told me not to take him back in the first place. I did not want to look like a fool.

I called my sister, still in tears, and I asked if I could stay at her place? She said yes, then she asked me what was wrong? I told her the whole situation, and she said, "You have to stop letting him walk all over you and let him go; he means you no good. He is doing nothing but using you, bringing you down, and stealing your youth. Every other day it's something with this guy, and you need to wake up before it's too late."

Sniffling and wiping my tears away, I replied, "I know, but it's hard because I love him," to which my sister said, "Well, what does love have to do with it? Actions speak louder than words. He doesn't really love you if he just wants you to keep going through this with him." A part of me already knew that, but I was speechless at that moment.

One part of me needed to let him go on without me. The other part of me couldn't. He needed me, and so I thought, it was like having a devil on one shoulder telling me to 'stay, he will do you right eventually,' and an angel on my other shoulder saying, 'you are too good of a person to keep dealing with this – run now while you can.' I was stuck between a rock and a hard place.

I have always been a patient and kindhearted person who has always given people the benefit of the doubt. I knew that he had a good heart and genuinely cared about me, but he just could not handle things when he was put in a stressful situation. I believed that all he needed was a little guidance and help to get his life back on track. If we could just make it to the ATL, I thought, then maybe things would get better with a change of scenery and a job he loved to do.

The next day he came calling me with fake apologies, which I knew he would. This had, in fact, become a recurring cycle of his. I really didn't want to hear the excuses he had to tell me now. His conversation began with him telling me that he had gone over to his father's house earlier that day, and they had had a drink which had caused him to act that way. I told him I was tired of his 'not caring about anybody's feelings' type of behavior and that he needed to change his ways. "I'm not going to keep putting up with this when you decide to get drunk. You need to grow up. I no longer care about how sorry you are or the million excuses as to why you did what you did or continue to do what you do. Come on, man, you need to get it together, you have a good person standing by your side, and you are draining the life out of me." Again, he promised he would change, and oh boy! He was indeed a good manipulator. I once again got taken in by his apologies!

When we were finally prepared for the yard sale, we ended up having it in the basement of his place instead. We had a great turnout and made $500 for the stuff we sold over the course of three days. That was not going to be enough to get us to the ATL, though, plus our eating and living arrangements until we found a place to stay. We had to try to come up with more money. The lease at his place was going to be ending soon. After it ended, we didn't plan on re-newing, so we just stayed at a motel until we were ready to move out of town. We were hoping to leave right after Thanksgiving.

We had all these plans with not enough resources to do any-thing, and staying at the motel was not cheap or a good option. I worked a few extra hours at my job to help pay for the motel, and he continued to work as a pizza delivery driver, hoping that he would get large tips. On days that I didn't work my job, I would ride with him to deliver pizzas to the customers. I had to keep talking to him about his drinking and driving especially while working. I thought we had got over this? But I guess not.

He acted like a man-child who needs to be told over and over again as if he doesn't know any better. I had not signed on to babysit a grown man. I asked him, "Do you really want to lose your job? We are sacrificing a lot to leave town to make a better life for ourselves. You can kill yourself or an innocent person and go back to jail. Is that what you want? Then, what are you prepared to do? You are not going to learn your lesson until something bad happens. Please just put it away." He did without argument or hesitation. I said, "You can't keep doing this to us. It's about time you take control of your life as nobody else can do it for you–only you are responsible for your actions." I continued to tell him how much I loved him and cared about what happened to him and if I didn't, I wouldn't be here wasting my time with you, and all he could say was, "I know."

The feelings weren't reciprocated. I was waiting on him to say the same things about me or at least say thank you. "I'm just a knucklehead who keeps messing up," he would say. "I'm a work in progress, but I will try harder to do better." I listened to his words, but in my mind, I already knew it wasn't going to be that easy for him to change, and I was right.

He once told me stories of how he would go out to restaurants and would never leave a tip, and even when he ordered pizza, he never gave a tip to the delivery driver, but now since the shoe is on the other foot, he understands how important tips can be when you are only making three dollars an hour. Since he had a record of being in prison, this was one of the few jobs he was able to do at the moment until he could get to this new job at the gym in the ATL.

I witnessed one of his schemes firsthand while riding along. If a customer used their credit card to pay for their food, he would deliver their food and have them sign their receipt. Most of the customers would leave the tip box blank, so that gave him the opportunity to add a tip amount on the line, and that was how he made a lot of his tips. I guess people were like how he once was; they probably didn't realize how important tipping is either. I told him that he was wrong for doing that, and it was stealing anytime you take something from someone without asking, but he ignored me and continued to do it anyway.

I did not want this to be something we would argue about because for the first time in a long time, we were actually getting along with one another, working together trying to accomplish a goal, so I did not say anything else, but still, I did not agree with what he was doing.

Working at a hotel which was my job, brought many benefits, like being able to put in a request to be transferred to another location once we moved out of town. I had worked there for over a year, so I did not have to reapply for a position. I just had to be there in person to do a face-to-face interview. I contacted two hotels in different locations that were on the transfer list, and both of them told me that once I moved there, to call and schedule the interview. I was so excited I could not wait to move; I had been dreaming about moving to the ATL for a long time.

I attended community college for Recording and Arts, and all I wanted to do was write, produce and make music that people would love and have it heard by the right people. I wanted to become multi-talented with my music. Those were my intentions and dreams before he came into my life. He promised to help me get my music career started and everything; well, let's just say that never happened.

We were in a good place with our relationship. We were back to being intimate with each other. Having sex became very painful for me after my abortion and I didn't know why. Our sexual experiences had never been painful before. I decided to schedule an appointment with a gynecologist to find out what was going on with my body. I wondered if I really hadn't healed properly or if something might have actually happened from the procedure. I went to the appointment, and the doctor told me that I was probably just experiencing irritation from dryness and I should use a lubricant to help with the dryness.

I bought the lubricant, but when we used that, it started to burn me in my vaginal area. I told my boyfriend how it felt, and he didn't seem concerned. He demanded that I just deal with it. I did not want to, but I did it anyway. Sometime in about the middle of July, I noticed I had not started my normal menstrual cycle, which would have been due by now. I mentioned it to my guy, so he bought me a pregnancy test, and I was like, here we go again. The home pregnancy test was positive, so I went back to the clinic just to make sure the home pregnancy test had been accurate. I found out that I was officially pregnant, and he was very excited.

In some way, I felt like I owed this to him since he would constantly remind me that I killed our first unborn child by having an abortion. I would completely beat myself up about what I did. I thought that maybe now having a baby would change his life, make him a better person and that it was the last piece to the missing puzzle he needed to make him whole again or to make his life make sense. I know I can overthink a lot, and this was another one of my naive thought processes.

I told a few people at my job whom I normally talk to about me being pregnant, and they were in disbelief. "Again? Are you going to keep the baby this time?" one of my co-workers asked. I said, "Yes." "Well, are you going to tell your parents?" I said, "No, not until I move out of town." I was so scared to tell my parents because of everything I had recently gone through with the first pregnancy that I aborted, and now, I turn around and get pregnant again.

My co-worker told me I shouldn't do that to my parents; I wasn't sure about how I would tell them. 'They are going to be very upset with me,' I thought. She said, "You have to tell them as you wouldn't want them to find out after you leave town. That is just not right." I responded by saying, "I'll think about it."

At the same time, my sister was also pregnant with twins. I remember when she called me and told me she was having twins, we both were in shock; she never thought about the possibility of having twins. Once I was pregnant again, I did think about the idea of if I was pregnant with twins. The thought of my sister having twins made me want twins, too, silly me. I talked about in the beginning how he wanted a little girl, and he still did. Every morning he woke up, he would ask, "How are my two girls doing?" I'd be like, "What if it's a boy?" So, we would joke around a bit, but he kept on saying it was going to be a girl.

As time went on, we couldn't afford to continue staying at a motel. We tried living out of the limousine, but that just didn't work. He decided that it was best if he went to live with his father, and I thought I would go live with my sister, that way, we could actually save money. He eventually sold his limousine for two thousand dollars. That was huge for us; that amount of money could really help to boost our finances for this move. When it rains, it pours.

Just when I had thought things were looking up for us, he called me to inform me that half of the money was gone. I asked, "What do you mean it's gone?" He said he had it put up in his suitcase and now it's not there. I said, "Check again. Did you check everywhere?" He said, "Yes," I asked, "How much was missing?" He replied, "$1300." I could not believe this. I was mad as hell. He said he believed his adopted sister stole it since she was still living with their father as well. He confronted her, but, of course, she denied it. Although we never found out the truth, or maybe I just didn't know the truth, we weren't able to do anything but accept what was left, which was seven hundred dollars. I could only hope it had nothing to do with him lying to me or some type of addiction.

It was almost time for my sister to give birth to her twins. It was a boy and a girl, so we were excited, and I was 3 months pregnant by that time. One of our cousins was hosting the baby shower, but my sister ended up going into labor two days before the shower, so it had to be postponed. My niece and nephew were born in September of 2007. My cousin rescheduled the baby shower sometime after the twins were out of the hospital. It was still a pretty good turn-out, and my family was able to meet the babies. I was four months pregnant at the baby shower, not showing yet, and my parents still didn't know.

During the baby shower, one of our cousins spoke to me and said, "I heard that you are having a baby too." My mom was sitting right next to me, and she chimed in and said, "NO, SHE'S NOT! She isn't pregnant," I froze. My heart was pounding so hard and fast, almost coming out of my chest. I replied that I was not pregnant, and my cousin had this blank stare on her face and she said, "Oh, I thought you were." My mom said to her, "You got that wrong." What a mess, I was almost caught, but I didn't know how to feel then.

I eventually told both my mom and dad that I was pregnant before we left to move out of town. They were hurt and very disappointed that I would lie to them and put myself back into the same situation I was trying so desperately to get out of. My father said, "I loaned you the money to get the abortion, so you wouldn't have to deal with that situation, and you went right back and let him talk you into getting back in the same predicament." He said, "Alright, you're grown now, and you have to learn how to be an adult, so I'm done with it."

I was sad that I had let my parents down, and it was extremely hard for me to tell them what they weren't expecting to hear. I just felt so bad about everything. Before leaving for the ATL, I paid back my father all the money he had previously loaned me. I put in my FMLA early so I could have time to get hired at one of the hotels once we got there. The hotel's Human Resources department allowed me up to 60 days once I delivered my baby to transfer to one of the locations there.

On Thanksgiving Day, we spent our last holiday with his family. That was my first time meeting his entire family. I had only known his father, brother, sister, and aunt, who owned the bridal shop. It was nice how everyone made me feel welcomed. It was also comforting to know that they approved of our relationship status. I am normally quiet and shy around people until I warm up and get to know them. It took little to no time to get accustomed to his family.

They talked to me all night, made me laugh, and were asking questions about how we met, the pregnancy, about us moving out of town together, etc. I couldn't believe that this was it, that we were finally moving to the ATL. As the night came to an end, we hugged and said our goodbyes. We went home, packed up, and loaded the car for our long trip the next morning. I was leaving town and my old life behind at 5 months pregnant, on a road trip with a long travel ahead.

Destiny

What's meant to be will be. I needed to follow my heart to see where my destiny took me. I'll be feeling no sorrow and looking forward to tomorrow. I've been on this journey for a while. Let's continue to see it through till I begin to smile. Confused and abused in reality – that's what I was feeling. I was alone in my zone, afraid of asking for help. Trying to live my life but ultimately paying the price. I have no doubt that if I knew then what I know now, I wouldn't have gone that route. But alas! Destiny has its mysterious ways that you can seldom foresee!

ATL, HERE WE COME! I was so excited to leave home and move out of town to start new beginnings and refresh my life with my man and our unborn child. I was also ready to continue what I had started with my music career. When we arrived and settled, everything seemed to be going well. Nothing could have prepared me for the storm that was about to come.

We hadn't thoroughly thought things through. Arriving in the ATL was surreal, but we really didn't have a stable place to stay; we just weren't prepared. We left home with only seven hundred dollars in our pocket and what we could fit in the car. That wasn't enough to spend on a motel for a week or to feed ourselves. Things were more expensive now that we were here. We had no logical plan or clue what was about to happen. We knew for sure that he had a job waiting on him once he was ready to start working.

We ate ramen noodles, bologna, and peanut butter and jelly sandwiches every day to survive. We were definitely on a budget. Once he started his new job, he would get up and go to work every morning while I stayed at the motel alone. We had a lot of things to do once we had arrived. We needed to find me an obstetrician, get some prenatal vitamins, and check in with the Department of Job and Family Services to apply for food vouchers, W.I.C. for the baby, and health insurance. I still needed to set up a job interview for the hotels I had chosen to transfer to before leaving town.

About a week and a half of him working and us living in the motel, he met someone at the gym who had been looking to rent out one of their homes. We were broke from spending all our money to stay at the motel, and he hadn't got his first paycheck yet. She wanted first and last month's rent as a deposit, and she was leasing the house for $600 a month. He explained our situation, and they worked out an agreement for us to move in. She gave us two months to get our money together. My guy knew it would be difficult to pay for everything by himself, but he was going to try, and he had appreciated all the landlord's help in giving us a chance.

I knew life would be challenging here, and it was at first. He would meet many different people to get advice and ask his clients if they knew of any good doctors who delivered babies. One of his clients recommended a midwife who actually delivered babies. I began seeing her once a month, and she prescribed me the prenatal vitamins that I needed. We had also gotten all our affairs together, so we could accomplish everything we needed to.

I had scheduled an interview with both of the hotels. The day came for the interview, and he took me to both appointments. He told me to make sure I let them know that I was currently pregnant so that they wouldn't be surprised if they did decide to let me transfer there. I really hadn't planned to mention anything because I did not want it to be a disadvantage for me not to transfer to either one of the locations. Even though, according to their policy, I had 60 days after having my baby to try to find somewhere to transfer to before the company would terminate my employment permanently.

During the interview, I mentioned that I was pregnant like I was told to do but did not get either job. I don't know if that played a part in my employment situation or not. I had wished that I hadn't told them until after I was back working, but we live and learn from our mistakes, making us better prepared for life. I felt that he had given me bad advice, but it was my fault for listening to him. I should have followed my first mind. I told myself, 'I'll try to interview again after I have my baby. I still had time, but I would soon learn that time doesn't wait on anyone.'

After about a month of living in the ATL, things started turning sour once again. He had started to slowly creep back to his old ways. Yelling at me for completely no reason, physically abusing me, punching holes in the walls, and drinking heavily. I told him, "I thought we had left town to start anew and to leave your demons behind, but you just brought them with you." I wondered whether I had really just made the stupidest mistake by moving down here with him knowing how rocky our relationship had been previously.

We had our good days and bad days, but more of the bad than good. I would cover the holes he punched in the walls with different celebrity posters that I had brought with me. I was hoping that it would conceal the holes if our landlord stopped over to collect the rent. I told him to stop punching holes in the walls because this was not our property, and if the landlord saw this, she would probably put us out, and we had nowhere else to go.

When I left town, my father told me that he had nothing else to say. He was mad; he wouldn't speak to me. He didn't reach out or call me to see how I was doing or how things were going in the ATL. I spoke with my mom whenever I could, and she said that my father hadn't changed his mind about talking to me. I spoke to my sister often. She checked in on me regularly, making me happy and feel like somebody still cared. She did not want me to leave with him either and still didn't like the fact that I was continuing to see him. Still, she showed me love and never ever turned her back on me. That's what you call a big sister. "THAT'S MY BIG SIS," and she has always looked out for me no matter what. All I wanted to do was prove my family wrong about him and, most importantly, prove to myself that I made the right decision. **Did I make the right decision? Only time will tell.**

He started to introduce me to everyone as his wife. That's what everyone knew me as, and he made sure everybody knew that we were about to have a baby. Since we were still new in town and didn't know too much about the city, he would ask his clients and co-workers about things such as where he could find stores to buy maternity clothes for his wife because she was pregnant.

Although we hadn't found out the sex of the baby yet, he would like to get suggestions of baby names from people every day. He would come home from work with a few different baby names every night. It was only girl names that he would tell me. I asked, "What about boy names?" He said, "We are having a girl. I know it," I said, "OKAY, if that's what you believe."

We went to our ultrasound appointment as planned to find out the sex of the baby and also to make sure that the baby was still growing healthy with no problems. The ultrasound tech said, "Everything looks good, and by the way, congratulations! **It's a girl**," His eyes got big, he was all smiles, "I knew it," he replied. "I told you it was going to be a girl." I was happy. I had gotten to the point that I didn't care if it was a girl or boy as long as the baby was growing correctly and was healthy. He was smiling from ear to ear. He was thanking the ultrasound tech. I'm like, "What are you thanking him for? I'm the one carrying the baby." He turned to me so he could kiss me, and he then said to me, "Thank you for giving me what I had wanted for a long time."

I was happy that she was healthy because some days, I wouldn't feel like eating from being so stressed out, but I always made sure to take my prenatal vitamins. We heard a commercial on the radio about offering 3D ultrasound images to see how your baby would look before you give birth. It was an optional service that you needed to pay for out of pocket if you wanted to have it done. We decided to pay for the image just to see how she would look, and she looked just like her dad in the ultrasound photo. It was amazing; we couldn't wait for her to be born to see if it was accurate or not.

One of his clients told us about a program where you can do bible study and earn points toward getting items for your baby, such as; a stroller, a crib, clothes, etc. We decided to drive there to check it out; it was 45 minutes away from us. The place was nice. It had a lot of items we could get with the points that we earned, and the staff was friendly and very welcoming.

The bible study consisted of doing homework assignments of our choice, and I had to turn the homework in weekly to earn points toward baby items. The more homework assignments I completed, the more points would build up for me to get bigger items such as; a crib or a swing. He began to work only half a day on Fridays every week to take me there, and I picked up new items, which helped a lot because we didn't have anything for the baby. I was even able to get myself some maternity clothes with the points.

We befriended a couple we met at the bible study program. They were lovely people and had two little girls. We talked to them often and invited them over to our place. He barbequed, and we had a good time with them, and it felt nice for a change for us to enjoy ourselves without arguing.

The landlord and I had also become good friends. I would walk to her house. She lived right down the street from us. Although we were friends, I knew she trusted him, and I was scared to say anything about who he really was. I would often hang out there while I was still pregnant and while he was at work. She sold Mary Kay cosmetics, and she would have Mary Kay meetings that she held once a month, and I would go with her sometimes. He worked 16 hours a day, 6 days a week, except on Fridays when he worked half a day.

Hanging with the landlord gave me something to do in the meantime so that I wasn't lonely. He would leave for work at 5:30 am and wouldn't get home until 10:30 pm. He had taught me the basics of cooking so I would have dinner ready for us to eat together when he came home. After a while, I started going to work with him. I would get on the exercise bike and watch T.V. while he worked. His job was to sell training packages to clients.

It was fun at first being at the gym. I met all types of celebrities, such as; hip-hop rappers and actors/actresses who would come there to work out. I hadn't been focused on my music because of the pregnancy, and I stayed so stressed out about our situation I just couldn't keep my mind on the music. Every chance I got, I would write poetry, though. I started writing poetry when I was 17 years old after my great-grandmother passed away. I considered her to be one of my best friends. Writing was like medicine; it helped me cope with and express my feelings, so whenever I felt down or overwhelmed, I would just sit down and write.

After a while, I got bored with going to the gym, and all I wanted to do was stay in the house. It was now around January of 2008, and I was just getting bigger. I was 7 months pregnant by this time. I was driving us home from his job one night, and I mentioned to him how I really did not want to go to work with him anymore just to be sitting around all day. I'm getting further along in my pregnancy, and I get so tired and out of breath a lot now. I want to be able to lay down and sleep. He got so mad that he told me to pull the car over. He got out of the car, walked over to the driver's side and yanked me out of the car, and said, "I'll drive, get on the passenger side." I said, "You didn't have to yank me out of the car. Was all of that really necessary? What's wrong with you? I'm 7 months pregnant." He tells me to shut up and just get on the passenger side.

At this point, tears started rolling down my cheeks. I kept praying in my head for God to help me through this. I zoned out like I did once before. The next thing I knew, I was jumping out of the car as we had come to a stop getting off the freeway. He was screaming, "What's wrong with you? Are you trying to die? Get back in the car." I'm yelling back, "I might as well be dead. It's not like you care."

With no family or no friends here, who could I really talk to? I wasn't even working.

I left my family to make a better life here with this man. I told him, "This was supposed to be a fresh start for the both of us, and I can't do this with you any longer. I am mentally, physically, emotionally tired of this lifestyle." He was still yelling, "Just get back in the car," so I got back in the car, and we drove home. I was full-blown crying at this point, saying, "I am tired... I am tired. Why do you keep treating me like this?" He continued yelling at me, saying, "You make me do this. It's your fault. If you stopped pissing me off, I wouldn't have a reason to put my hands on you." "How is it my fault? All I said was how I didn't want to go back to the gym because I am getting bigger and further along in my pregnancy, and I am getting tired and out of breath a lot now, then you have a fit."

"What part of I'm pregnant don't you get? You're the one who wanted a baby so bad, pressuring me into having a baby, and you're about to make me lose this one with all this stress you're putting me under. I am literally about to lose my mind. I don't know what you want from me. You say you want a baby, and now I'm pregnant, you wanted a girl, and your prayers were answered. I'm having a girl, but you're still not happy. I don't know what to do anymore."

Everyone I knew here were all his friends or people he knew. These people were his co-workers, his clients, the landlord, and his buddy, who helped him get the job at the gym. I was even scared to talk with our neighbor who lived across the way from us because, of course, he was friends with him as well, but I believed that the neighbor knew what was going on. The neighbor just never said anything to me. I had ridden with the guy's wife to the store a few times, so I didn't want to say anything about my situation to any of them. I figured they might be loyal to him or that they would tell him that I said something and someone could get hurt because of me. I did not want that to happen.

"Why do you hurt me rather than talk to me?" He said, "You're right. I'm sorry I was way out of line." We have been going through so many problems throughout our entire relationship. He said he has this book called the Seven-love Languages that is supposed to help couples learn how to communicate with one another through the seven-love languages. I said, "We need to read that book together and try everything it suggests because all this arguing and putting your hands on me is getting old, and I don't want it affecting our child."

One night he didn't come home. I constantly called his phone with no answer, so I became worried. The next morning, I received a collect call from him, and he said, "I'm in jail," I say, "Jail? What happened?" So, he explained to me that when he was on his way home from work, our street had a checkpoint where the police were stopping cars and checking to see if drivers had a driver's license and insurance.

Unknown to me, this man had been driving on a suspended license. I asked, "Why did you never tell me this?" He told me that it happened when we were back home when we argued. I had left the house, so he went out after me, and the cops pulled him over and found an open container of alcohol in the car, so they gave him a citation and told him he could dispute it in court. He did not show up to court, so his license was suspended. I was so pissed off that he would keep that from me.

"You drove us all the way here and continued to go back and forth to work on a suspended license?" He said, "I knew that you would be upset, and he really knew how I felt about him drinking and driving." I said, "You still should have told me you put both of our lives in danger, being selfish. I could have gone to jail also. What if I was driving the car and the police pulled me over? Would they have automatically assumed I had been drinking and the alcohol was mine? These police officers can be ruthless, and they do not care who you are. I have never been locked up or put in that type of situation before."

When the police arrested him, they impounded the car. He had contacted his friend, who he reached out to when we had moved here, and luckily, he was a retired secret service agent. His friend called me to let me know that he would take me to pick up the car and pay to get it out of impound. My guy had to stay in jail for 3 days before he could be released, in the meantime, I didn't know what to do without him, so I started cleaning up around the house. We both had our own bathroom. That's where he would go to smoke his black & mild's, be alone, or use the toilet. He only used the other bathroom that was mine if he needed to shower because the other bathroom, he always used only had a toilet and sink.

As I was cleaning the house, I started finding empty beer cans like 40/40 and hard liquor bottles such as gin, his favorite alcohol. I found some in his bathroom behind the toilet, in our spare bedroom closet, under and inside the sofa, and even in his gym bag that he takes to work with him. I was furious. By the time I was finished collecting all of them, it had turned out to be a mixture of 26 empty beer cans and hard liquor bottles combined. I placed all the beer cans and liquor bottles on the kitchen counter for him to see when he got home. He had already known how I felt about him drinking and lying about it. He had previously told me that when we left to come to live out of town, he would try not to drink as much, and I was hoping he would stop completely.

It was time for me to pick him up from jail, and I didn't say a word about the empty alcohol cans and bottles I found due to his excessive drinking. When we got home, he walked in and passed by the kitchen counter, not noticing what was left on the counter for him. He sat down on the sofa facing the kitchen counter, so he couldn't believe what he saw when he looked toward the kitchen. He had no idea what I had found. He couldn't say a word. He just shook his head.

I said, "Really! This does not make any sense at all. I found 26 empty beer cans and liquor bottles that you hid from me. Did you think I would never come across any of them? Or figure you out?" I told him a long time ago that he was an alcoholic and needed help. He denied being an alcoholic. He said, "I told you before that I drink when I get stressed." So, since that's all the time, I said, "That makes you the perfect candidate for the job. How many times have you told me the same old same old? How many times have I given you the benefit of the doubt?" I said, "Again, you need help. It's different if you were just a social drinker or had a drink every so often, but you are a habitual drinker. I know you have been drinking at work again because I found bottles in your work bag. Are you trying to lose your job? We can't afford for you to lose your job while we have a baby on the way."

Manipulation

You put a spell on me. Always manipulating my mind and then corrupting me with your lies. Me believing them, but why? You were clever; however, your spell is starting to fade, and now I can see past your charade. Thinking it was simply a phase while you were treating me like your slave, manipulation always has its way.

Chapter 5

March 25th, the day before my birthday, I drove him to work as I saw that he needed me to. I thought I was just dropping him off, then going back home to relax, then coming back to pick him up when he got off of work. I was nine months pregnant by this time. I was tired and exhausted by just being pregnant. When we got to his job, I parked the car to let him out. I told him that I was going back home to rest and to call me before he was ready to be picked up, but he flipped out on me. He said, "You're not going anywhere; we don't have enough gas for you to drive home and come back later to pick me up."

Then, he went on and on about how I was trying to make him lose his job by doing so. I asked, "What are you talking about? How and why will I try to make you lose your job? You already know that I do not want to sit here all day, as it'll put a lot of strain on my body, but you act like you don't understand when I keep telling you this!" He started going off the deep end and screaming at me at the top of his lungs, so I laid my seat back and just sat in the car all day, listening to music until he got off from work. I went inside only once to use the restroom and then came back out to the car.

I was living in hell every day; that's how I felt. I wanted so badly to leave this relationship, but I didn't want to be a single parent if I didn't have to. At this point in time, it was no longer about me loving him anymore. I wasn't in this relationship mentally or emotionally; I only stayed for the sake of our child, even though she wasn't born yet. I needed his help until I could get up on my feet, so I dealt with him. That night when I went to bed, I woke up at about three in the morning to use the bathroom, and I noticed that he wasn't in bed. He left me a note on the floor in the hallway that read, "I am going to the store, and I'll be right back." I shook my head and said to myself, "The store, huh, at this hour of the morning."

I proceeded to call his cell phone, but it rang and rang with no answer. I hung up and called right back, and this time a female police officer answered. The officer told me that they had him in custody and also told me that they were doing a driver checkpoint, and one of the officers signaled him to stop, but he wouldn't, and he drove past three officers, so they had to chase him down. The officer then said that they were going to impound the car and I could go pick it up in the morning.

I pleaded with the officer saying, "Please don't take the car. I'm pregnant, I don't have any family or friends here, I'm not working, and I don't have any money to get the car out of the impound." The officer said, "I will have the tow truck bring the car to you, but you need one-hundred and five dollars to pay for the tow." I kept on telling her that I did not have any money, then I remembered when he got paid, he did put up hundred dollars to my name just in case of an emergency. I told her that I only had hundred dollars, and she said, "Let me ask if that's okay with the tow truck driver," and the driver said that it was okay with him, thankfully.

I waited outside for the tow truck to arrive. The tow truck driver came with the female police officer who I had spoken with on the phone. The police officer pulled up in the driveway and got out of the cruiser, and was holding up a little bag. She asked me, "Do you know what this is?" I looked at it and said, "No." She stated that it was crack cocaine, and they found a bag of it in the car when they pulled him over. She asked me if I was smoking with him as well. Again, I said, "No," and that I didn't know he was either. The officer told me that I needed to leave him because there was something seriously wrong with him, and I should be thinking about my baby. I looked at her tearfully and said, "Okay."

When she left, I walked over to the tow truck to get the car, and the tow truck driver said, "That's a shame; what man leaves his pregnant wife at home to go and get something like that?" I was so embarrassed and ashamed of myself for being with this man, let alone about to have a baby with him. I was so angry and hurt at that moment that I couldn't even think clearly, and honestly, I was done living like this and dealing with all of his mess.

The next day when I got a call from him in jail, I said, "I had no idea you had been involved with that type of stuff, and you told me, once we left Ohio, you were done selling it as well. Why do you continue to lie to me and do such things behind my back!" He claimed that a friend of his needed a ride, and when he dropped the friend off, the friend must have dropped the substance in his car. My response was, "You left a note telling me that you were going to the store. WHY DID YOU LIE?" He couldn't answer the question. I asked him, "How would I ever be able to trust you when you continue to lie? The police officer told me what happened."

He swore up and down that he didn't know that they were sig-
naling for him to stop. I had heard enough of his lies and hung up the
phone on him. I thought, if the police officer was telling me to leave
him alone, then I really needed to consider leaving him and going
back home. She didn't even know him or me or what I had been going through with him, and in no time, she formed an opinion and
could tell that something wasn't right. A friend of his picked him
up from jail and dropped him off at home for me. I was trying not
to hear it anymore, but I just had no other options at the moment. I
was going to be giving birth soon, and yet, I was still arguing with
him. Oh, what was I to do!

A week later, on April 10th, we went to our final Lamaze childbirth class. Shortly after the class was over, I started to have some
cramping pains in my stomach. Two weeks prior to the 3D ultrasound, they had determined that my due date would be April 24th,
so I didn't think there were any serious concerns. I couldn't take the
pain any longer as he drove me to the hospital. I was scared. I didn't
know what to expect since this would be our first child, even though
I read parenting books and took childbirth classes.

When we arrived at the hospital, we had them call our midwife.
They put us in a room and gave me some pain medication while we
waited on our midwife to come. I thought that maybe I was going
into labor, considering how bad the pain was. When our midwife
arrived, she examined me and told us that I had only dilated 1 centimeter. She had me get up and walk up and down the hallway to
see if that would help me dilate more, but that didn't help, and I was
still at 1 centimeter and becoming increasingly nervous. She told
me to go home and pack our bags, then come back to the hospital
later that night.

We arrived back at the hospital that night. Our midwife was called and notified we were back. She came to check and find out how far I had dilated, but it still wasn't enough, so she left the room. I did not want to be in pain when trying to push out my daughter; I wanted to have an epidural done. It took the doctor three times to get the needle into my spine correctly for the epidural. My baby's dad asked the anesthesiologist if there was a problem, "Why are you taking so long getting the needle into her back? How long have you been doing this?" The doctor answered, "I have been doing this procedure for fifteen years, but this is the first time I have had this problem." I was finally sedated and able to relax and sleep until it was time for me to deliver the baby. "It's the way her bones are structured that is causing the difficulty, and she needs to have it assessed at her follow-up appointment," he said.

About an hour later, I heard the nurses running into the room screaming my name, saying, "Wake up! Wake up!" but I was still drowsy from the medication, so when I opened my eyes, my vision was blurry. I felt a vibration on my stomach, and I heard my child's father asking them what was going on. They said, "The umbilical cord is trying to wrap around the baby's neck, so the vibration was helping to reposition the baby." Some of the nurses were on break, but they had monitors in the cafeteria, so they were able to check and see what was going on, and when they heard the alarm, they all came running.

After that ordeal was over, we both fell back asleep. Our midwife came again around 7 a.m. the next morning, April 11th, to see how far I had dilated. When she left that night, I was 7 centimeters, and when she returned that morning, there still weren't any changes. She told me that they would have to do an emergency C-section or the baby would drown inside me. I was scared and nervous, and I didn't want to be cut open, but she made me feel comfortable when she told me it wasn't going to look bad; it'll just be a cute little bikini split that I wouldn't even notice.

They prepped me for surgery, and two hours later, on April 11th, I delivered our healthy baby girl at 9:50 a.m., weighing 5lbs 15.8 oz. She was finally here, and I was excited and anxious at the same time to actually meet her. I didn't know if I would be a good mom since this was all so new for the both of us. Our midwife even took a picture of us while my daughter's father was holding our little bundle of joy, standing next to me while I lay on the operating table as I could not move.

Once I got back to my room, I finally spoke to my father; I called him and told him that his granddaughter had arrived. He asked how she was doing and how everything had been going; we talked on the phone for a while. The couple that we met at bible study also came to the hospital and brought us fifteen big bags of stuff like; baby clothes, diapers, wipes, etc. I was so happy and thankful because we couldn't afford much. We basically had nothing besides a crib, swing, stroller, and a diaper genie that we were able to get from bible study prior to having our daughter. My daughter's dad left the hospital and went home for a little bit. He said he'd be back later that night. I said, "No problem."

All day I tried to get my daughter to latch on to my breast so she could be breastfed, but she would not latch on. The hospital did not have any breast pumps available, so they had to order one for me. I was still exhausted from surgery, and I really wanted to rest, so they kept my daughter in the nursery, and the nurse bottle-fed her formula in the meantime.

That night my daughter's dad called me and was acting strange and paranoid. He said he happened to look out the window and noticed a car parked outside our house and that they were watching him. I said, "Huh, what are you talking about? Who is watching you?" He said, "The FBI." "Why would they be watching you?" I asked. He said, "I don't know, but I am too scared to leave the house to drive back to the hospital at this time of night." I was upset. I didn't know what he was talking about, so I said, "Alright, don't come." He could tell I was upset, so he said, "I'll try to come once they leave, don't worry about it," I replied, "Okay," and then hung up the phone and went to sleep.

I stayed in the hospital for four days after the delivery because of the C-section surgery. The breast pump they ordered came before I left the hospital; it was a hand breast pump, and I had to follow the instructions and learn to use it myself. He didn't come back to the hospital until the day I was discharged with our daughter from the hospital. The hospital prepared us a going-away meal that we ate before we left; it was delicious.

You

You, that's all I can say. You, stole my youth. You, took my life away. You, damaged my spirit and my soul, then swallowed me whole. You, did this to me. You, made me weak. You, told me nothing but lies and made me realize that you were a devil in disguise. You, that's all I can say. You, took my life away.

Chapter 6

A few weeks had passed since our precious daughter was born. The feeling that I was a mom was now so surreal. As the days went on, nothing had changed between us. He was still being himself, still doing the same dumb stuff, including taking my house keys, locking me out of the house, hiding my cell phone charger, and not fastening our daughter in the car seat properly. He would literally put the car seat in the back seat of our car, with our daughter in it, but not strap the seat belt on or across her. Those are just some of the evil things he would do.

I would argue with him constantly about him being so irresponsible, and his response would be, "But we're only going up the street." I would say, "It doesn't matter. Anything can happen. We can get into a car accident in that split second; safety comes first. Just because you don't care about your life, try thinking about someone else's life for a change."

When she was two months old, I had enough of the abuse from her father. I knew it was time for me to protect her from what I had dealt with in the past. I called my mom on the phone, crying, begging, and pleading for her to send me enough money to buy a Greyhound bus ticket to come back home. She asked me how I would get to the bus station if she paid for the ticket. I didn't know, but I told her that I would ask my neighbor. I wanted all these things done so I could leave while he was at work because I didn't want to argue about it, him trying to stop me from leaving or us getting into a fight.

I went across the street to ask one of our nosey neighbors, and he told me that he did not want to get involved since he still had to live here and he did not want any trouble with him. I said, "Okay." He then insulted me by propositioning me, asking if I could perform oral on him, then he would give me a hundred dollars. I said, "No thanks, I am not interested," then left. I went two houses down to ask my other neighbor if it was possible for her to drop me off at the Greyhound station, and she said sure with no hesitation.

I was taking only the things that I could. I even left him with my car. I got my things together, ready to leave. While we were on the way to the bus station, my neighbor asked me why I was leaving. I told her the truth. She said, "Something isn't right with him and plus, you are so young. You are doing the right thing because you do need to think about yourself and your baby and get as far away from him as you can." I listened and agreed. I really didn't say much else because she was right, but I did still love him, and we had broken up and gotten back together so many times. This time was different, though. I knew I had to leave him for good because we had a child now. I couldn't continue to let her be around that negative energy and see the way her dad was treating me.

I was very appreciative and thanked the lady a lot while getting out of the car. I proceeded to Customer Service with my baby and my things to pick up my one-way bus ticket back home that my mom had already paid for using her credit card. It was a struggle trying to carry the car seat, my suitcase, and her diaper bag at the same time, but many people helped me along the way.

Once I finally got settled in my seat on the bus, my phone rang, and it was him. I answered it, and he asked, "Where are y'all at?" I said, "We are gone," He said, "Gone! What do you mean gone? Where y'all at?" "On my way back home where we belong," I stated. He screeched, "What! Y'all better get back here now." I told him that it was over, things hadn't worked out the way I thought they would, and I spent a lot of time being naïve, and I am a mom now, and things needed to change," I also said to him "You are not going to continue to talk to me like a child or treat me like one." I told him that I wasn't about to keep putting up with his nonsense and anger issues, and then I hung the phone up on him.

He repeatedly called and texted me, but I ignored him. I continued to think about what my neighbor, who had dropped me off, told me. I thought about what the police officer had told me before I had my daughter. I thought about what my parents and sister kept telling me and how my life had changed so much. Everyone had my best interest at heart when they were trying to warn me, but I refused to listen. My family forewarned me not to leave with him in the first place. I thought I was being an adult by making my own decisions, and they were the wrong ones. But I had just been taken advantage of and made a fool of because I was so young. I was in love, I thought, but I had no idea what real intimate love was supposed to be.

My father picked us up from the Greyhound station. I was happy to be back home and away from that devil and his abuse. I was also happy that my family was finally able to meet my little bundle of joy. Getting settled in back at home, I ended up living back with my sister, who I stayed with before I left town. Her twins at this point were nine months old, and my daughter was two months old. The twins were seven months older than my daughter, and my sister also had an older daughter who was five years old at the time.

I began looking for employment right away. My father told me about a hospital that was doing a lot of hiring and that I should apply. I was applying for all types of jobs every day. When I wasn't getting any calls back from the employers, I had nothing but time on my hands to keep thinking about the guilt I felt for leaving. I had forgotten about the opportunity with my previous employer. After having the baby, I never did try to re-interview for the hotel position, so since I was back home, I visited them and got a signed notice from the human resources department that stated I was on FMLA. I had a few months left, so if I could not find a job within the time frame that they had given me, I would be eligible for unemployment until I found another job.

In July of 2008, a month later, of me being back in my home-town, I finally spoke with my daughter's father, who was pleading with me to reunite with him. He told me that he was sorry and tried to convince me that he'd never do it again. He also told me that he was going to church now, and the house is not a home without us being there. It had taken for us to leave him before he had realized how much he needed us to complete him.

I took a few days to think about what he said, and I called him and told him that I'd come back, believing that he honestly meant what he said this time. I figured with us being miles away and not with him for a month, that would give him time to miss us and think about what his actions had caused. You never know what you have until it's gone, and he had to learn that the hard way.

This time he paid for the tickets for us to catch the Greyhound bus back to him. I began having second thoughts, but I assumed that this had been a wake-up call for him. I hoped that he had realized how close he came to losing his family, and that would have gotten his act together.

As soon as we arrived and got off of the Greyhound bus, he ran up to us and gave us the biggest hug, "I missed y'all so much," he said. "I messed things up," he repeated. "I almost lost y'all," and he thanked me for coming back to give him another chance. I told him that it was hard for me to forgive his actions, but I hoped that he meant what he said this time. I did not want any problems from him, and he promised me that things were going to change and be a whole lot different.

He said, "I see you gained some weight, and your butt got bigger," I smiled and said, "Yes, all I did was eat while I was home." He laughed and said, "You know I like a big booty, so it doesn't bother me." It did feel good being back in the ATL but, I just did not want to see any of my old neighbors especially, the neighbor who drove me to the bus station with my daughter, she had told me that I should not come back and I did not want her to judge me. I sort of felt embarrassed and ashamed for coming back.

We settled back in, and he helped me to unpack. We sat outside on the porch and enjoyed the weather, and then we went to pick up something to eat. Everything was going well; it had been a couple of days since we were back.

I should have known that things wouldn't be good for long. Things between us were too predictable. I was just sitting back, waiting to see when he was going to strike again. We had only been back two days before everything turned sour once again. Things had gotten even worse than they were before I left. I regretted ever coming back to try to work things out, but I really wanted my daughter to grow up with her dad.

He was outside cutting the grass one afternoon, and I was in the house with the baby, so when he was finished outside, he came in the house trying to pick a fight with me. "Here we go again," I said to him. He got all up in my face, and at that point, I said, "I should have never come back; I knew in my heart that you were never going to try to change." I was trying not to argue with him in front of our daughter. That's not the life I wanted her to know at such an early age.

I got our daughter ready for bed, and we went to sleep early that night to avoid any problems.

My normal day-to-day routine was to wake up when he woke up for work so that I could iron his work clothes and make his breakfast. I was such a committed homemaker that way. After our falling out last night, I didn't do any of those things. He said to me, "I guess you aren't going to iron my clothes and cook me breakfast today, huh?" I didn't say a word; I acted as if I was still asleep and didn't hear him.

After he got ready and left out for work, I woke up and got myself and my daughter ready for the day. I really needed to get out of the house and go for a walk and get some fresh air to clear my mind. It was a nice day to be outside, so I fastened her into the stroller, and we walked to the movie theatre that was just a mile down the road from us.

We still only had one car, so he drove back and forth to work himself, even though he wasn't supposed to be driving because his license had not been reinstated. Ever since the baby had arrived, I was busy with her, learning to be a new mom, so I didn't have the time to drop him off and pick him up as I had done before.

He decided to call me while he was at work to say that he really wanted to apologize to me for how he acted yesterday. He told me that I didn't deserve to be treated in such a bad way, but the neighbor that lives across the way from us made him mad, and he took his anger out on me. I replied, "Why can't you just do right by me for a change?" What blew me away, though, was when he said, "Oh! Somebody gave me these pills to take, and I was in the sun far too long after I took them, so the sun must have triggered the pills to make me moody." I responded with, "WHAT? You are such a habitual liar. It's always an excuse with you. Please tell me why do you continue to do the things that you do? I love you so much, but I am so tired of dealing with you when you act like this. You tell me that things are going to be better if we come back, and we're back, but you haven't even given us a whole week to be here before you start tripping." He said, "Please don't leave again. You aren't going to leave, are you?" I said, "Honestly, I do not even know, I haven't decided yet, and this time if I do, I won't be returning."

As the rest of the week went on, things were good enough between us that we could communicate without arguing. He suggested that we should start going to church every Wednesday night, so we did. He would leave work early every Wednesday to pick us up for church because church services started at 6:30 pm.

Two weeks into going to church, we met a friendly couple there who were much older than the couple we met at bible study. Actually, they were probably closer to his age. The wife said that she was a school teacher and that her husband was a truck driver. We exchanged phone numbers, but we never hung out with them as we did with the other couple.

I did not have access to their phone number since he took control of everything. He had run the other couple away because he was constantly asking them for money. I'm sure they started to feel as if they were being used, so I guess they got tired of it, and we never heard from them again. I was hoping that he didn't do this couple the same way. I told him that he was an able-bodied person who needed to stop begging so much, but he continued to say, "Well, we need the help; that's why I do it."

One day, our daughter wouldn't stop crying, and her body felt extremely warm, so I took her temperature, and the thermometer said 104 degrees. I immediately called her father at work and told him, hoping that he would leave work early to take her to the emergency. Instead, he gave me the phone number of the couple we met at the church and told me to call and ask if one of them could take me to the hospital. I called, and the wife answered the phone. I explained who I was and asked her if she could take my daughter and me to the hospital because she wasn't feeling well and her father was at work and he had the car. She said sure. I gave her the address, and she picked us up and drove us to the hospital. She was only able to drop us off and couldn't stay because she told me that she had somewhere to be. I said, "Thanks for the ride; hopefully, her dad can come pick us up once we are done here."

I checked my daughter into the E.R. She had calmed down from crying at this point but still had a fever. They called us to the desk and asked me some questions about what had brought me there, then took us to the back to check her temperature again, which was still reading 104 degrees. They immediately put us in a room, and the doctor came in shortly. They checked my daughter out fully, including her ears, and ran some tests. The test came back positive for an ear infection, so they gave me some medication to give to her daily until it was finished; I was relieved to hear that it was nothing more serious.

After the emergency room visit was over, I called my daughter's father and told him that he needed to pick us up. I told him that she had an ear infection, and he asked me, "How did she get that?" I told him that the doctor said that when water gets into babies' ears and sits there, it can cause an ear infection. I always wash her hair when I bathe her, so the doctor told me to just be careful not to allow the water to drain into her ears. He said it would be another hour before he could leave work and asked me to call the lady back to see if she would be able to come back to drop us off at home. I called her, and she was able to come back for us and take us home. I told her how grateful I was for her help and thanked her for everything.

I had applied for unemployment, and they denied me. My hotel job had told them that I terminated my own employment with them, but that had been a lie. I had proof that they allowed me to take FMLA early and maternity leave. Once my baby was born, they told me if I did not find employment within one of the hotels during the time frame that was given, I would be eligible to file for unemployment; that is exactly why I went to the hotel's human resources office to get a notice stating what they had said and had them sign it when I was back home just in case.

I appealed the unemployment and sent them the paperwork affirming what was told to me from the hotel, and about a week later,

I was approved for unemployment. I didn't receive much money; I was only getting three hundred dollars once a month. I still had to look for employment and call the hotline weekly to verify that I was indeed searching for employment which was the requirement to allow me to continue to receive payment from unemployment.

Every morning, I would walk to nearby stores applying for jobs with my daughter in her stroller. If I had to go online to do the application, I would take the bus to the library to use their computers and internet service. I went as far as going to the employment center to see if they could help me find a job. I was determined, but I had no luck.

I was glad to be getting a little bit of money coming in so I wouldn't have to keep asking her dad, but it still wasn't enough to help with the majority of the bills; it was just enough for us to go buy groceries. At times he couldn't afford to pay the car note, and the car was in my name.

One night while we were sleeping, I heard a noise, like something was being dragged on the ground. It was around 2 a.m., so I got up out of bed and looked out the kitchen window, and saw it was our car being repossessed. I woke up my daughter's dad and told him that the car was being towed. He jumped up, ran outside, and banged on the window for the tow truck to stop. He asked, "Why are you towing our car?" The man said that it is getting repossessed and he is only doing his job. My child's father asked the tow truck driver if we could get our stuff out. The man said, "Sure," and asked us for the car key so that he could put the car on the tow truck correctly. My child's father went into the house to get the car key and came back outside, handing the key to the tow truck driver, and we grabbed all of our stuff out of the car, including the baby car seat.

My daughter's father was pissed. He asked, "How am I going to get to work now?" I was upset as well because he was supposed to be taking care of the car note payments, and I didn't know that he hadn't paid the car note in months. Now we were stuck without a vehicle, and the repossession was going to be on my credit. He had to be at work at 6:30 a.m., so his only choice was to call around to see if one of his friends or co-workers would be able to pick him up and drop him off at work until he figured out what his next steps would be.

At that moment, a part of me had wished that we had never even moved out of town. To begin with, I would still have a car, my job, and a reliable place to stay. All I could think about was how I had a good job, and I lost it being with this man and letting him turn my life upside down. I would have been so much further if we had never dated, and I probably would have finished college with my degree. If I knew then what I know now, I would have listened to everyone when they told me not to leave, but at this point, it was what it was. I couldn't turn back the hands of time, so I just had to continue to move forward.

As time passed, things were getting harder and harder for us financially. He couldn't afford another car, so he had to continue to find a ride to and from work or catch the bus. On the weekends, it was more difficult for him to catch the bus because they ran once every hour and, on the holidays, the bus didn't come down our street at all. He had to walk quite far up the hill in order to catch the bus when he needed to.

He had no idea how to manage his money. Without the car, he had to pay out of pocket a great deal of his money to people who would take him places or for bus fares. He wasn't paying the bills like he should, so our electricity kept getting turned off. I would have to go next door to a neighbor's house to ask if I could warm my daughter's bottle up there. I would walk down the street to the movie theatre when it was extremely hot just to be in air conditioning for a while when our electricity was turned off. He borrowed money from his friend that helped him to get the job at the gym and again from one of his clients to who he had sold a training package at work.

I asked him where all his money was going? He said, "You know I work off of commissions, so if I don't sell a certain amount of training packages, then I don't get a bonus, and that's why my checks don't amount to much." I told him that maybe we should try to apply for some assistance with our light and gas, and he agreed. We had planned on going to the place early in the morning, but when I woke up and got him up to get ready so we could go, he said no.

I asked, "What do you mean no?" He told me to leave him alone. I said, "We've already talked about this, and we agreed it was what we needed to do." He said again, "I told you no, I'm not going," and I needed to leave him alone. Then he took the pillow that he was lying on and threw it at me. I said, "Was that really necessary? I am trying to help our situation, and you throw a pillow at me." I don't even know why I'm surprised by his action since this is who he was. He did dumb stuff like this constantly. I said, "Forget it. I am about to go to the store to get our daughter some more formula." I took a shower and got dressed, then I got my daughter dressed, and we left the house.

I walked to the store, which took me about 30 minutes, there and back. When I returned home, he was standing on the porch waiting for his ride to take him to work. As I was walking up the driveway, he was walking off the porch to get in the car. He had the house door closed, so I looked in my purse to get my house keys out to open the door, and my keys weren't in my purse. I yelled, "Where are my keys?" He yelled back, "The door is open!"

When I went inside and got situated, I called my dad to tell him about what had happened. He said, "You need to stop letting him walk all over you," I said, "I know." I called my sister after I got off the phone with my dad, and she told me the same thing. She said, "You should have never gone back," I said, "Yeah, I know."

Later, that night when he got home, I and the baby were still awake. I was lying on the sofa watching her play with her toys. She had just started learning how to crawl. I turned my head for a second, questioning her father about why he took my house keys out of my purse. When I looked back over at the baby, she was holding something in her hand that was really tiny. I jumped up and grabbed it out of her hand and walked over to her father, and said, "Look at what she had in her hand. What is it?" He took it from me and said, "Let me get rid of it," He walked into the bathroom and flushed the toilet, then came back in the front room and said, "It was a rock." "As in crack?" I asked. He said, "I don't know how it got in the house," "What do you mean you don't know?" I asked. "So, it just appeared out of thin air and landed on our living room floor, huh? You are the only one that could have brought something like that into this house. What if she had put it in her mouth? Then what? She could have been poisoned. We could have gone to jail for child endangerment and possibly lost custody of her. Do you want that to happen? I thought you were done with using and selling? Once again, you just disappointed me. Please, don't bring your bad habits into this house anymore."

He shook his head and apologized. He said he wasn't thinking clearly, and that was very irresponsible of him, and he must have dropped it there when he was using. He promised he wouldn't ever let anything like that happen again. I replied, "Thank God that I saw it before she had put it in her mouth." He wanted to redirect the conversation, so he reached into his pants pocket and pulled out my house keys, and handed them back to me. I didn't say anything. I didn't even have the energy to continue arguing after what had just happened.

The next day he went to look at a car that someone was selling. It was a stick shift, and he knew how to drive a stick shift, but I didn't. He said he would teach me how. He purchased the car, and the guy allowed him to make monthly payments on it. I waited and waited for him to teach me how to drive the car, but he never did. He told me I didn't need to learn anytime soon because I didn't have anywhere to go. I said, "I still have to go to the store to buy formula and pampers for the baby." I told him that it was important for me to learn because you never know what might happen and also so I don't have to keep asking him to take me places, and he said, "Oh, I can take you wherever you need to go." I told him that he needed to stop trying to control me. "Since I've come back here, things seem to have gotten worse, and your behavior is unbelievable toward me." He just looked at me and didn't say a word because he knew what he was doing.

When we originally moved into our house, he wouldn't make me a house key without me asking continuously. It took some time before he actually made me a key of my own, but he never expressed why. He never once stated that he wanted the house keys back from me, so why would he go into my purse without my permission and take them away from me? Is this man trying to control my every move? Now he buys a stick shift car knowing full well that I don't know how to drive it. Why is he so vindictive? I've been dealing with mental, emotional, and physical abuse from him constantly. I'm living this painful life every day. Why can't I just walk away?

Sunday was the day my daughter's dad was usually off from work. He would take the baby outside on the back porch to play with her so that I could have a break from my mom duties and give me a chance to catch up on some well-needed rest. I was lying on the bed in our bedroom, and it was dad's day with the baby, but he kept calling me to come watch her crawl as if it was something she had never done before. I said, "She's been crawling for a while now, and I've seen it already." I can still remember when she used to scoot on her head trying to crawl, it was the cutest thing. He had never witnessed her crawling, only the scooting on her head she used to do, but now she was crawling well. I said, "I'm exhausted, and I'll come look later or another time," He said, "Come now." I said, "NO!" He got so upset that he slammed the patio door as if he wanted to break it, then he came into the bedroom and got in my face and said, "If I said get up, then you need to get up." I said, "You need to stop talking to me like that. You are not my daddy."

Once again, he took his fist and punched a hole in the wall and then told me, "That's why your family members would beat you, and that's why nobody liked you at your old job." All these negative things, I had actually confided in him, but I didn't know that he would use my words and the situation that I was going through against me every chance he got. I went and grabbed my baby which he left her outside on the patio porch and I laid her on the bed with me, just to make sure he didn't hurt or scare her. He had a very short temper, and it took the littlest things to set him off, and that wasn't good. One of those off days turned out to be a day I had wished he went to work.

Our daughter had started walking when she was only six months old. Everybody was so excited for her but couldn't believe how advanced she was especially since she had started crawling at four and a half months. She was starting to eat table food as well, and I had started trying to wing her off of her pacifier. Her father wasn't happy about that because she would cry all night, and he had to go to work in the morning. He would say, "Just give her the pacifier to shut her up," I said, "NO! She has to learn to sleep without it, she is six months old now with two teeth, and I do not want her sucking on the pacifier any longer." It took her about a week before she really got over wanting her pacifier.

Last Time

This is going to be the last time, and I do mean the last time. Have you really lost your mind? You must have, treating me like a piece of your property, like you're my master back in the times, stressing me so much I had to rewind. Looking back on the situation, it was true, yes, I was naïve and blind but, that still didn't give you the right to mistreat, disrespect, and abuse me. You definitely crossed the line Oh, but you can never do it again because this was your last time.

Chapter 7

It was Christmas day, and the year was 2008, our daughter's very first Christmas. We weren't able to buy gifts, so my morning plans were to wake up and cook holiday dinner. I wasn't a good cook, so almost everything I made came from a can, and my daughter's father cooked the chicken on the grill. He didn't eat beef or pork, so I never had to cook that. I wasn't against it myself; I just didn't cook it at home. I needed us to be able to see eye to eye for the sake of our daughter, so I asked if he would comply and just spend time as a family, and he said he would like that.

Things were going well thus far. The weather was nice outside, maybe 80 degrees or so. I called my family to wish them a happy holiday and to brag about how we were outside on our deck barbecuing while they were in the middle of a snowstorm. As the day went on, I noticed he started to get agitated, but I didn't speak about it or really think much of it because of our agreement. I went back into the kitchen to finish preparing the food, and he had finished barbecuing at this point, so we were ready to sit down and eat. I suggested that we watch a movie. He said, "We can. I'm just going to run around the corner really quick to a friend's house," and I asked, "For what?" He said, "I just have to take care of something," I asked, "Well can we come with you?" He told me no and to stay home and finish cooking. I said, "I'm done. It wasn't anything serious, just canned food."

In the back of my mind, I already knew what he was doing, but I also wanted to hear what his excuse was. I wanted to hear him say it. I had hoped he wouldn't ruin the holiday for us, but I figured he wanted to sneak and go behind my back and have a drink as he always does. At that moment, I instantly caught an attitude, it was Christmas, for goodness' sake, and you're supposed to be here with your family. I definitely knew that something was not right.

"I am so over you and this relationship, so just go," He told me to come and sit down so we could talk. I responded, "No! We do not need to talk about anything since you said you were leaving, so just go." He said, "We need to talk," I just ignored him. He came into the kitchen, where I was, and got up in my face like he always does, and I told him to move away from me. He said, "No, we are going to talk," I said, "I do not want to talk now," He pushed me up against the refrigerator, grabbed me by my shirt, and swung me from the kitchen into the living room, then threw me on the couch and sat on me. I screamed at him to get off of me. "I can't breathe; get off of me!" He had me pinned down for at least a minute before he finally got up.

I jumped up and grabbed my daughter, and went outside to sit on the porch with tears flowing down my face until he left. As I was sitting on the porch holding my daughter, I kept praying to get out of this situation. After about five minutes, he came out the door to where I was and told me that we were going to talk when he returned, so I stood up to go back into the house, and he put his hand on my shoulder to sit me back down in the chair and continued to say to me, "Like I said we are going to talk when I get back home."

After that confrontation, I just went back inside the house and continued crying. I didn't even have an appetite anymore, so I fed my daughter what I had cooked and put the food away. This was her first Christmas, and I couldn't get over how badly it turned out, but it was a good thing that she was young and didn't understand what was going on. I still had to be a mom to her even though I was really stressed and depressed after the whole situation.

It was still early, around 6:00 p.m., but my mood had changed, and all I wanted to do now was sleep. I gave her a bath, put her pajamas on, and rocked her to sleep. After she fell asleep, I laid her in her crib and started to clean up the kitchen. Then, I took a shower and got myself ready for bed.

Before I headed to bed that night, I wanted to call my parents to tell them what had just happened to me, and I noticed my cell phone needed to be charged, so I started looking for my charger and could not find it. He came walking through the door, and I asked him if he had seen my phone charger. He told me that he had hidden it under the bed. I asked him, "Why did you do that?" He never responded. I said to him, "Anything could have happened to our daughter or me, and I would have no way of calling for help." He talked to me and apologized like he always does about how he's been treating me and how I don't deserve that. Just the same conversations over and over with no change. Enough is enough, I thought. What would it take for me to leave his life for good? I really wished I had never met him at all. He ruined my whole life and the dreams and goals I had set for myself.

During his talk to me, after all his apologies, he said he would like for us to go to church on New Year's Eve to bring in the New Year fresh. I said, "No, because things have not changed. I thought that since we were going to church together every Wednesday that it was supposed to help our relationship become better, but it didn't. You keep saying it, but you need to do better. You keep pushing me away, so if there is not going to be a change for the better, I'm going to pack up and leave again for good and never look back. I gave you chance after chance after chance, and you don't appreciate me or my kindness, and you don't even show me that you really love me. I don't know how to feel about you anymore. You have ruined my life with all your craziness and addictions since we've met, but yet, I stay. This is not what our daughter needs." He replied, "I know I'm going to do better; I promise." I told him that promises are meant to be broken and that he has broken all of them, and it's time for more appropriate actions, not promises.

I still had my refills of the prescription for Vicodin, a pain medication that my doctor prescribed to me after having my daughter via C-section, so every night, whether we argued/fought or not, I would take three pills just to numb the pain of everything that I was going through. I also wanted to be asleep before he got home from work so I wouldn't have to deal with him, and the pills would help put me to sleep. I became addicted to taking the medicine for that reason only, and it just became a part of my daily routine. Sometimes I would hope that I didn't wake up. I was contemplating suicide throughout this whole ordeal of our relationship. Some days were worse than others. Even after I had my daughter, suicide was constantly on my mind.

I need to leave him alone for good, I kept saying the same thing over and over, and I know that is why he continues to treat me the way that he does. He doesn't believe that I will leave because he knows that all he has to do is apologize, and I'll forgive him as always, and if I do leave, I'll just come right back. He had gotten rather comfortable with the same routine, so he wasn't really trying to change.

This is not the life I wanted to live. I don't want our daughter growing up in this type of environment and believing that it's okay for a man to put his hands on a woman or, for that matter, her father putting his hands on her mother. I have put up with this abuse for two and a half years by myself but now that we have a child together, I don't want her being involved. I have to protect her.

New Year's Eve came, and we were doing good the last few days. I was hoping that this was really going to be a new beginning for us. We went to church as planned and brought in New Year's (2009) together. He hugged us and promised that things were going to get better from here on out, and I believed him as always. A whole hour hadn't passed before we got into another argument right after we left the church. We've just had a conversation about how you had been acting toward me, but you continued with your broken promises. I prayed and prayed to God for help, to make things better, but all I wanted now was an out from this relationship.

Dear Diary

Dear diary, today is the day for me to leave and get away. I have to think about my daughter and how to keep her safe. This man means us no good, so why do I stay? He has hurt me deep within my soul and killed my spirit unconditionally, so much so that I want him to feel the same way I so desperately want him to pay. I've prayed, and I've prayed, I forgave, and I forgave. The pain has hurt me way down to the core, to an extent that the love I had for him has turned to hate. Dear Diary, my mind and my body have started to feel so numb that I can feel the tingling in my thumb. I have to get away before I die today. My daughter is counting on me, so today shall be the day.

D on't get me wrong. We've indeed had our good times together as well! Those good times are what I think about
when I decide to stay with him and fight for our relationship. Unfortunately, the bad days seem to outweigh the good days.
There have been times when he treated me like a queen and would
be very respectful toward me. He was a smooth talker, but it was his
sense of humor and overall personality that did it for me – I knew I
was going to love him.

In the beginning, when we had met, I wasn't looking for anything special, but as time went on, I began longing for a relationship
with him. He was such a keeper; he had won my heart. He made me
laugh and smile and seemed like a real grown, mature man, just like
someone I had always wished to spend my life with. I just knew I
could count on him to take care of me.

He was my ideal and a Mr. Wonderful, I would say. We spent
quality time together; he would run my bath water for me, he would
cook for me and take me out for dinner, when possible, he would
find someone who could do my hair and nails, and he also introduced me to his female co-worker so that I wouldn't have to sit at
home or the gym all day alone before I had the baby. He also asked

one of his gym clients if she was available to hang out with me or have a lady's night out, and we did. She was really nice. She would pick me up from my house, and we'd go to the movies to see Dream Girls when it first came to the theatre. On different occasions, I went over to her house to chill. Sadly, for me, we never exchanged phone numbers; she always contacted me through him.

So, as I said, we had good times as well; at least you get an idea of why I stayed. Why has he changed, though? Was it because of his addictions or just a fake disguise to draw me in? Sometimes you think you really know someone, but you have no idea who they really are in reality. That seems to be the case, but I loved him so hard that I couldn't wrap my head around who he really was, and instead, I only saw him and rather idealized him as who I wanted him to be. I felt like I would make things work even if it killed me. I didn't want my daughter to know him this way, but I didn't want her growing up without him either, so I gave him many chances to love me like he used to or maybe, pretended to.

Our third anniversary was coming up on February 16, 2009. Although that wasn't the official date that we became a couple, it was the date when we had rerun into each other, so we decided to make that day our anniversary. I wanted to surprise him with a gift since the money had been so tight lately, and we both had been under so much stress that we hadn't shared anything, and maybe that was why we were drifting apart, I thought. I didn't know what I should buy him, but I wanted it to be memorable yet, affordable.

I remembered that I had picked up an Avon book a while back at a store. I started looking through the book, and I came across men's cologne. That's what I can get him! I told myself. It was a cologne by Derick Jetter, and at the time, I didn't know who he was, but they had the scratch and sniff sticker in the book, and his cologne smelled good. So, I called the phone number that was given in the book and placed an order. The Avon representative came to my house two days later to drop off the cologne, and I paid with the money that I was getting from my unemployment. She wrapped the gift up good, and I hid it in our bedroom closet until I was ready to surprise him with it.

February 14, 2009, Valentine's Day, was on a Saturday that year, and I remember it like it was yesterday. As usual, he had work, but he told me that he would try to get off early so he could make me Valentine's Day dinner. I thought that would be lovely. Our daughter was sick with a head cold, so I spent all day trying to get her head cold under control. She had a bad cough; she would gag every time she coughed. Her dad usually got off from work at about 10 or 10:30 p.m., but he came home around 5 p.m. that evening.

He came into the house, got situated, and then started preparing the dinner he had promised me. He told me to stay in the bedroom until he finished cooking, but somehow, he ended up burning the food. He came into the bedroom and said, "I messed up!" I looked at him with a blank stare, confused, waiting for him to tell me what he had messed up. He looked at me as if he was waiting for some affirmation to continue, so I asked him, "What did you mess up?" He replied, "I burned the food! I had the fire too high, and it burned." He then suggested, "Maybe I'll just order Chinese food," and I replied, "That's fine."

When the food arrived, he brought it to me, and we sat in the bedroom to start eating. Our daughter had started coughing and choking really bad, so I jumped up, handed her to her dad, ran into the kitchen to put some water in her sippy cup, and then came running back to the bedroom. I took her back from her dad while she was still choking and tried giving her some water to help clear her throat. He jumped up and stormed out of the room, and I asked him, "What's wrong with you?" He replied, "I was going to go get the water for her," I said, "Really, it didn't matter who went to get the water; she was choking, and I wasn't about to sit there and decide who was going to get up and get her some water. So, you're mad over that? Really! That is so childish!"

As I held our daughter and let her drink the water from her sippy cup, he got in my face and raised his fist toward me as if he would hit me. "Get out of my face; you always know how to mess up a good mood!" I told him. He then told me to make him get out of my face. I said, "I am not going through this with you again. Get out of my face," He then told me that he was leaving.

Once he left, I was able to calm her cough down and then got her ready for bed. I laid her down beside me, and we fell asleep. About 12 o'clock midnight, he came walking through the door, came into the bedroom, tapped me on the shoulder, and said, "Hey! Can we talk?" I said, "I don't want to talk right now; we are sleeping." He said, "We need to talk now," I said, "No! I am not talking to you right now." So, he got into the bed, and when he did, he purposely snatched the cover off our daughter and me. I grabbed her up and started yelling, "That was so uncalled for! I will sleep on the air mattress in the living room." He jumped up behind me with our daughter in my arms, pushed me out of the bedroom, and slammed the door. When he pushed me, there was a wall straight ahead coming out of our bedroom, so her head almost hit the wall. I had to shield her with my hand, which still hit the wall, to stop her head from hitting it instead.

I went and laid her on the air mattress and then went back into the bedroom to retrieve my cell phone because I had a habit of sleeping with my cell phone under my pillow since I never knew what to expect from his behavior. I said to him, "Don't you ever put your hands on me again!" I then grabbed my cell phone from under my pillow. He jumped up out of bed in a rage and pushed me on it before he started choking me, so, at that point, I was fighting him and yelling at him to get off of me.

It had gotten so loud that our daughter woke up and crawled into the hallway where she could look into the bedroom, and she started crying hysterically while she watched. I fought her father off of me; I went into the closet, got out his anniversary gift, and showed him. "I was trying to surprise you for our anniversary," I said, "And now I'm definitely gone." He smacked the bag that the gift was in out of my hand, picked it up off the floor, and threw it at the wall, breaking the cologne bottle.

I went to grab my daughter and call my parents like I always do to let them know what was going on at our house at one o'clock in the morning. He kept denying that he had put his hands on me. He kept saying that I was lying on him and that he did not touch me. "Why would I call them at one o'clock in the morning if you didn't try to choke me?" I replied. My mom said, "You need to get out of there and come back home," I said, "I know, but it's hard to leave. I don't want to be a single parent trying to raise our daughter on my own." My father advised, "If you don't leave now, he will end up killing you, and your daughter is going to have no choice but to grow up with no parents."

For the rest of that night, or shall I say early morning, I thought about leaving him for good and not coming back this time, but I was scared of being a single mother having to raise my daughter by myself. I thought about what my father had said, and it was definitely time, though. I was tired of all the abuse and mistreatment. That morning he didn't go to work. I woke up and was shocked to see him still at home. I got our daughter up so I could feed her breakfast when he came and snatched her out of my arms. I said, "Give her back to me; why would you do that?" He replied, "I want to spend time with my daughter today." While he had her, I went to get in the shower. I had a lot on my plate, and I was just going to take her for a walk while I thought about what I wanted to do. I got our daughter back from him, and he asked, "Where were you going?" I said, "For a walk," he asked, "Where?" I said, "None of your business," He then told me that I better not take his daughter away from me again.

I was sitting in the chair as I got her dressed, and her father suddenly got in my face and asked me again about where I was going. I said, "Get out of my face," He said, "Make me," and before I knew it, I slapped him in the face. He stood up and went to lay down on the sofa. After I got her together, I put my purse under the stroller, and I proceeded to head out the door. He jumped up and said, "You aren't going nowhere," and then he grabbed the stroller and pushed it over toward the couch, so I grabbed our daughter out of the stroller and walked out the door.

I was fed up with him. He started following me and telling me to get back inside. I got to the end of the driveway, and he grabbed my right arm, which almost made our daughter fall. I said, "Get off of me," He said, "Don't make me cause a scene out here." I said, "Go ahead; that's probably what we need at this point."

I started looking around to see if anyone was outside. I looked up the street, and I saw our nosey neighbor who stayed directly across the street from us. He was up the street standing with about three or four other people, and I saw him looking down the alley at us. I told my daughter's father to get off of me while he was still holding my right arm, and I managed to pull my phone out of my back pocket with my opposite hand from where he was holding me, and I was able to call my mom. I told my mom that he was holding my arm and wouldn't let me go. She was yelling through the phone as though he could hear her. "Tell him to get off of you!" I said, "I did, and he won't." She said, "Well, call the police."

Eventually, he let go of me, so I started walking down the street with my daughter in my arms, so upset with myself, saying, "I should have never come back," still talking to my mom. My mom said, "I know you're an adult, but you and my grand-baby need to come home. You can't keep putting up with his abuse." She asked me, "What are you going to do?" "I'm going to go to the homeless shelter," I stated. My father chimed in and said, "No, you are not. Y'all need to come home now," and I knew I had to leave, but I didn't want to have to go back home to face the shame I felt.

My mom said, "You just need to think about your baby first." I turned around and walked back to the house. Our daughter had fallen asleep, so I laid her on the bed in the bedroom. I thought maybe if I showed her father that I was finally leaving this time that he'd do better. I didn't understand my own logic; why should I care now? He obviously didn't. I was dead set on pretending that I was leaving.

So, I went into our spare bedroom and started packing my clothes in the suitcase. He came into the bedroom and said, "That's my suitcase," and yanked the suitcase from me – it flew from the spare bedroom, where we were, and hit the door of our master bedroom where our daughter was sleeping. I said, "I told you that I was leaving. I'm tired of going through this with you, time and again."

I grabbed another suitcase, and he grabbed that one from me as well and threw it into the living room, knocking over the stroller. He left the bedroom when I heard the baby start to cry, so I went to check on her. I had forgotten that my purse and the diaper bag were still underneath the stroller. I calmed the baby down, and she fell back to sleep.

I went into the living room, and the stroller was still knocked over; I saw my purse lying on the floor along with the diaper bag. I picked the stroller up, including my purse and the diaper bag, and I noticed everything I had in my purse was gone. He had taken all my stuff. I had my driver's license in there, my social security card, our daughter's social security card, twenty-five dollars cash, and my unemployment card that had about a three-hundred-dollar balance; everything was gone. I had heard him go out the patio door earlier as I tried to calm our daughter down, but I didn't think he would have done anything of the sort.

I went into the master bedroom where my daughter was sleeping and called my father, explaining what had happened. As I explained the situation to my father, I heard the patio door open, and my daughter's father proceeded to come back into the house. My father said, "Go tell him that I said to give you back your stuff." I went into the living room, and he was sitting on the sofa and watching T.V. as if nothing had happened. I said, "Give me my things back," He said, "I don't know what you're talking about," I said, "Come on, give me my things back now." My father was on the phone saying, "Tell him I said to give you your things back." My daughter's father told me, "You need to get away from me. I don't know what you're talking about."

Upset, I went back to the bedroom, so my father told me, "Call the police," but I was too scared to do so. My father asked, "Do you want me to call the police for you?" I said, "Yes." My father asked me for the address, and I gave it to him. About ten minutes later, the police came knocking at the front door, I got off the phone with my father, and I went and opened the front door, and there were two male police officers, and one of them asked me for my name.

Once I told them my name, the officer said, "We received a phone call from your father; what seems to be the problem?" I was trying to explain what had happened when my daughter's dad spoke up and said, "I haven't done anything to her; she is lying about me," I said, "Really? You are the liar; you stole everything out of my purse." The police asked me, "Did you see him do it?" I said, "No, but we got into an argument over me wanting to leave, and I had my purse and our daughter's diaper bag underneath the stroller. He knocked it over, and once I realized it, my things were gone. He definitely has my things, officer." One of the officers said, "Well, if you didn't physically see him take it, then there is nothing we can do," They then asked me to step outside.

When I stepped outside, one of the officers closed the front door, so my daughter's father couldn't hear what we were talking about. One of the other officers proceeded to walk back to the police car while the other officer talked to me. He explained again, "If you didn't see him, take it, then there's nothing we can do." I said, "I don't feel safe here. Can you please take me somewhere?" The officer asked if I knew anybody that they could take me to. At the time, I couldn't even think straight, so I said, "No, I'm not from here, I don't have any family or friends here, nor do I work, he is the only one working right now, and I just had a baby almost a year ago." The officer said, "Well, if you don't know anyone here, there isn't anything we can do, try to stay in separate rooms for the night, and y'all probably just need to blow off some steam." I insisted, "But officer, I do not feel safe here with my baby and me in this house. He put his hands on me more than once," The police officer said, "We can talk to him and ask him to leave you alone, and y'all stay away from each other for the night." I said, "Really! This man can kill me, and there's nothing y'all can do?"

I went back into the house, and the police officer said, "Hey Yō," yelling for my child's father because he wasn't sitting on the sofa anymore. He came out and said, "Oh, I was in the bathroom." I went into the bedroom; the baby was still asleep, and then it dawned on me that I did have the church lady's phone number. I almost forgot that he gave me her phone number when I needed her to take me to the emergency when our daughter got sick. My cell phone had died completely. When I went to go plug it up, I saw one part of my cell phone charger plugged into the wall, and the other part was cut and lying on the floor.

I ran out of the bedroom to the police officer, who was still outside talking to him. I opened the front door and said, "He cut my phone charger, and my phone is dead." The officer asked, "Did you see him do it?" I said, "No, but he did cut it, and now I have no phone," He said, "If you didn't see him, do it, then there's nothing we can do." I looked over, and my child's father had this sort of smirk on his face, so I closed the front door back while the police officer was still talking to him.

I remembered the spare cell phone charger I had found back around Christmas time when he had hidden my cell phone charger previously, and my father had told me to put it up just in case he tried to do it again. "See, God doesn't like ugly – he tried his best to trap me," I told myself. I wasn't giving in or giving up anymore, enough was enough, and this was the end of the rope that held us together. So, I went and got the cell phone charger out and plugged my cell phone in so I could get enough charging to make a phone call.

I heard the front door open, then close, and I heard him walk over to the sofa area and turn the volume back up on the T.V. Then I heard him call somebody on the phone and tell them, "Yeah, she just called the police on me, and I didn't do anything. I was just sitting here minding my business watching T.V.," This is what he was saying to someone on the phone as if I was the troublemaker picking on him and making up stories. All I could do was shake my head. I thought to myself; this man is crazy; why did I even stay this long? I fell out of love with him a long time ago. I was basically trying to make things work for our daughter's sake.

While my cell phone was still charging, I was able to contact the lady from church to ask if she could come to pick me up. She asked, "What's wrong?" So, I explained what happened, and she told me that her husband's cousin had just come into town, and they were out eating and that they would be on their way. She told me to leave everything; she said, "Y'all need to get out of there. Don't worry about packing your bags, just you and the baby," She said she would call when they were pulling up. I said, "Okay, thank you so much," and then we got off the phone.

Thank goodness my baby had slept through everything that was going on. I still needed to pack my suitcase because I knew I wasn't coming back; this was it for me, and I didn't even have to think about it any longer. So, I packed my baby's diaper bag and half of her clothes, and I packed my suitcase as well with what I could fit in there. I placed my daughter in her car seat while waiting for the lady to call me.

Once she called, I grabbed the diaper bag, placed it around me, grabbed the car seat and my suitcase, and walked out of the bedroom. He was still sitting on the sofa watching T.V., looked over at me, but didn't say a word. The lady's husband's cousin met me at the front door and grabbed the car seat and suitcase from me, and I grabbed the stroller.

This was my first time meeting the cousin. As we pulled off, the cousin remarked, "Look at his punk butt looking out the window now. He's nothing but a coward putting his hands on a female. I want him to try that with me." He was mad about the whole situation and then said, "Nice to meet you and your daughter, by the way," This time, my daughter opened her eyes and looked around like where am I? We got to their house, and I thanked them again for risking their lives to save ours. They didn't know what kind of situation they were walking into, so I was so grateful that they came anyway without even knowing if he had a gun, a knife, or how dangerous the whole thing was going to be.

I was so scared that he was going to try to stop me from leaving, and really, I didn't know if he had a weapon on him myself. Once I got to their house, I called my mom, and she said, "When you come back home, you need to leave him alone for good and not have contact with him at all." I assured her, "I know, mom, and I won't." I have never wanted a broken home; I wanted a fantasy, but I kept telling myself that I could do this and that I'm not the only person who has raised a wonderful child on their own.

The next morning, the lady came to me and said, "Your daughter's dad called me, and he wants to talk to you. He wants to know if we can all sit down and talk." Then, she asked me, "Are you willing to do counseling?" I said, "No! I just want to go back to my hometown with my family," She asked, "Are you sure?" I replied, "Yes." She said, "Okay, that's good, because you need to think about you and your daughter," I said, "Yes, I know it's time that I do what's best for my child and me. He had many chances, and he blew them. I can no longer do this with him." She shook her head and replied, "I understand completely." She said, "You have your whole life ahead of you," I said, "I don't want my daughter growing up in this kind of negative environment."

The husband's cousin told me that he would buy me a Greyhound bus ticket back home. He was from out of town too, just visiting though, so he was leaving soon and going back home himself. I stayed two nights with them and also met their kids, who were all so nice. I felt good being out of that situation. My daughter's dad kept calling them, begging for me to talk to him, and they had to tell him to stop calling because I didn't want to talk to him. Then, he told them that we could not keep his daughter away from him and that he was going to fight me for custody, but they reassured me that it was just his anger talking, and with the track record that he had, he couldn't take my daughter away from me, and the courts would not allow that to happen. I knew that they were right, so I didn't sweat it.

The husband's cousin and I got ready to leave. The wife and her husband drove us to the Greyhound station, and off we went. While on the Greyhound bus, the cousin and I were talking, and he told me about his girlfriend, that she was pregnant, and so he had a baby on the way. He asked me about the situation with my daughter's dad, so

I told him, and he said, "That's not right. No man, no matter what the situation is, has the right to put their hands on a woman, period."

As we were talking, he leaned in as if to kiss me on my lips, and I turned my head and asked, "What are you doing?" He apologized and said he didn't know why he did that. I said, "Just because I am vulnerable right now doesn't give you the right to take advantage of the situation." He apologized again and said, "You are absolutely right."

We got off the first Greyhound bus because we had to switch buses. This time, we were on separate buses since we were headed to two different places. We said our goodbyes; I thanked him again for the ticket, and we parted ways. Now home for me was where I belonged, good riddance to my old life, but I didn't imagine that starting my new life would take so long.

Still, I Stand Tall

I've lived through all the struggles, battles and hard times.

I've been through it all and still, I stand tall.

I've experienced the hurt, the heartache and the crying.

I've been through it all and still, I stand tall.

The pain runs deep through my soul but I live
for my daughter who keeps me whole,

If it wasn't for her, I'll be dead and gone for sure.

I've dealt with this devil for far too long. I feel
so alone, don't know what to do,

I try to forget about what I've been through.

I've been through it all and still, I stand tall.

Love is so blind, that I didn't see what was right in front of me.

He kept apologizing and I kept forgiving.

Things had gotten so bad that I was tired of living.

I feel so-so blessed to get out when I did cause if I had stayed,

Who knows how things were going to end.

It was so hard leaving my life behind,

because I loved this man so-so much at that time.

The love was so true only to turn out to be lies but,

what he has done to me, we can never ever be.

I've been through it all and still, I stand tall.

Printed in the United States
by Baker & Taylor Publisher Services